THE DEEP ROOTS OF AMERICAN NEOLIBERALISM

Focusing on why neoliberalism gained such a unique strong hold in the United States, philosopher Bruce N. Waller in this book traces the source back to the country's origins and the entwined core values of the nation's Founding Fathers. Their extreme commitment to private property rights (as evinced in a unanimous vote for the Constitution's Fugitive Slave Clause), an aversion to widespread democracy, and a deep belief in the uniquely just nature of their new country together created the ideal conditions for neoliberalism's growth and success.

Waller also provides a clear analysis of the moral and psychological conditions so hospitable to neoliberalism, including the compatibility of faith in the "invisible hand" of the free market with the widespread belief – which remains prevalent in the United States – that the world is just and people generally get what they deserve. Waller examines how the ideal of moral responsibility in the United States provides the core belief that holds in place the basic principles of American neoliberalism. The book ends by shedding light on the deleterious effects of neoliberalism and shows that its replacement requires not only the amelioration of enormous inequity in wealth, but also the opportunity for all citizens to exercise autonomy, control, and critical thought in their lives and workplaces.

Key Features

- Traces neoliberal values deep into American history and culture
- Uses empirical psychological research to explain the broad appeal of neoliberalism

- Describes the strong interconnected neoliberal value system of belief in a just world, personal responsibility, and radical individualism, and their combined influence on American culture
- Examines the influence of neoliberal values on the American criminal justice and educational systems

Bruce N. Waller recently retired as Professor of Philosophy at Youngstown State University. His recent books include *Against Moral Responsibility* (2011), *The Stubborn System of Moral Responsibility* (2015), *The Injustice of Punishment* (2018), and *Free Will, Moral Responsibility, and the Desire to be a God* (2020). He is the co-editor (with Farah Focquaert and Elizabeth Shaw) of *The Routledge Handbook of the Philosophy and Science of Punishment* (2021).

THE DEEP ROOTS OF AMERICAN NEOLIBERALISM

A Cultural, Economic, and Philosophical History

Bruce N. Waller

Routledge
Taylor & Francis Group
NEW YORK AND LONDON

Cover image: © Zen Rial/Getty Images

First published 2022
by Routledge
605 Third Avenue, New York, NY 10158

and by Routledge
4 Park Square, Milton Park, Abingdon, Oxon, OX14 4RN

Routledge is an imprint of the Taylor & Francis Group, an informa business

Library of Congress Cataloging-in-Publication Data
A catalog record for this title has been requested

ISBN: 978-1-032-25719-8 (hbk)
ISBN: 978-1-032-25715-0 (pbk)
ISBN: 978-1-003-28468-0 (ebk)

DOI: 10.4324/9781003284680

Typeset in Bembo
by KnowledgeWorks Global Ltd.

CONTENTS

ACKNOWLEDGMENTS

I am indebted to many philosophers, psychologists, and legal scholars who have provided valuable insights into the material covered in this book. Very special thanks to Peter Alces, Gregg Caruso, Tom Clark, Michael Corrado, Paul Davies, Dan Dennett, Richard Double, Farah Focquaert, Robert Kane, John Lemos, Neil Levy, Gerald Massey, Elizabeth Shaw, and Saul Smilansky.

I am fortunate to have spent my academic career in a stimulating and supportive department, among people with profound understanding of many different areas of study who have been generous in sharing their knowledge: Chris Bache, Robyn Gaier, Michael Jerryson, Jeff Limbian, Brendan Minogue, Mustansir Mir, Deborah Mower, Gabriel Palmer-Fernandez, Tom Shipka, Linda "Tess" Tessier, Alan Tomhave, and Mark Vopat. Special thanks also to the amazing departmental administrators, Joan Bevan, Mary Dillingham, and Linda Glover who kept the department running very smoothly and efficiently. My students at YSU have inspired me with their dedication, energized me with their genuine delight in philosophy, and often amazed me with their insights.

I am grateful for the enjoyment and the enlightenment I have had from many lunches with Alan Jacobs, Jane Kestner, Ikram Khawaja, Jim Morrison, Tod Porter, and Charles Singler, and Mark Womble.

I have also benefitted from years of stimulating luncheon conversations with Fred Alexander, Luke Lucas, and Lauren Schroeder, concerning everything from ancient warfare to comparative religion to contemporary art, with fascinating detours into the negligible danger of being struck by a falling tree.

Thanks to Homer Warren and Linette Stratford for wonderful conversations and for introducing me to Producer Consciousness.

Special thanks to all the strange and wonderful members of the "McCauley Street Gang" from my Chapel Hill graduate school days, who have enlightened me on everything from the architectural design of Colonial Era barns to the origins of the U.S. Navy on Lake Champlain, and whose many years of deep friendship have been a special part of my life.

Marc Stratton and Andrew Beck have been very supportive and efficient editors, and Mohd Shabir Sharif did an excellent copyediting job.

Finally, my greatest debt and greatest joy is my family: my son Russell and his wife Robyn and their two wonderful children, Nathanael and Josephine; my son Adam and his husband, Joshua; our loving and playful poodle, Maggie; and my wife, Mary, a dedicated and brilliant psychologist who joyfully takes on the toughest cases, including me.

1

NEOLIBERALISM

Neoliberalism has a powerful influence around the world, especially in the United States and the United Kingdom. Though contemporary neoliberalism originated in Europe – primarily in Austria – in the mid-20th Century, the neoliberal system took root in the United States during the 1970s and 1980s. It gained followers among some economists, but its real power was in conservative political movements. *Why* did this invasive European species gain swift influence and sink deep roots in American thought? Framing the question in that way implies that neoliberalism is a radically new model that defeated and replaced traditional American beliefs and values. But the basic elements of neoliberal thought – "proto-neoliberalism" – have long been present in the United States. Neoliberalism is the contemporary manifestation of a belief system that has endured and flourished from the Founders to the present. Neoliberalism found a comfortable home in the United States because the fundamental principles of neoliberalism are deep American values.

The rise of neoliberalism is not a unique US phenomenon, but the United States and the United Kingdom are the settings in which it has had the greatest influence. The degree to which neoliberalism influenced other cultures is an interesting and intensely debated question (especially in Australia and Canada); but the focus here is on the rapid and deep adoption of neoliberal policies in the United States. The strength of neoliberalism in the United Kingdom is also impressive, and some common principles between the US and the UK versions will be noted, but the emphasis will be on the development of neoliberalism in the United States. What conditions made the United States fertile soil for neoliberal policies; and to what extent do those conditions still exist?

Contemporary neoliberalism emerged in the mid-20th century, the 1947 founding of the Mont Pelerin Society marking its systemic origins (though

DOI: 10.4324/9781003284680-1

of course its champions, such as Ludwig von Mises and Friedrich von Hayek, had been developing its doctrines long before). It has flourished in the United States and the United Kingdom since the time of Reagan and Thatcher, spreading its tentacles around the world through think tanks (including the Institute of Economic Affairs (IEA) and the Centre for Policy Studies (CPS) in the United Kingdom, the Heritage Foundation and the Ludwig von Mises Institute and the Competitive Enterprise Institute (CEI) in the United States, and the Institute of Public Affairs (IPA) in Australia), international monetary funds – such as the World Trade Organization (WTO) (Chorev 2005), the International Monetary Fund (IMF), and the World Bank (Babb and Kentikelenis 2018; Slobodian 2018) – and through political and military power. Its influence is worldwide, though the United States remains its strongest citadel. But some of the key ideas of neoliberalism have a much longer history, especially in the United States. Much of the neoliberal agenda was already present when the framers met in Philadelphia to draft the new Constitution of the United States – so much so that the United States might well be regarded as a "proto-neoliberal" culture from its revolutionary origins. The proto-neoliberal values of American culture made the United States a welcoming haven for a contemporary neoliberalism that had struggled for survival in Europe but flourished when transplanted to US soil.

Neoliberal Principles

Though different accounts of neoliberalism emphasize different features, David Harvey provides an adequate starting definition:

> the theory of economic practices that proposes that human well-being can best be advanced by liberating individual entreprenurial freedoms and skills within an institutional framework characterised by strong private property rights, free markets, and free trade.
>
> *Harvey 2005, 1–2*

Individualism, personal responsibility, celebration of freedom, and noninterference with the free market are basic neoliberal – and American *proto*-neoliberal – values.

The guiding principle of the neoliberal movement is the supreme virtue of the *free market.* Favoring a market economy does not make one a neoliberal: most people acknowledge the benefits of a free market when it operates efficiently and fairly. But neoliberal adoration of the market goes far beyond that. For neoliberals, the market is not merely a useful way of exchanging goods; it is the objective arbiter of values and the optimum source of knowledge. Hayek's grand neoliberal principle is that the market is the only path to objective *knowledge*: all else is mere preference or bias. The unified wisdom of the combined market far exceeds what can be known or understood by any individual. The free market is an impersonal force that collects all the fragmentary knowledge of its participants and produces the best possible overall output of material goods. Because this remarkable collective knowledge far exceeds the possible understanding of any person or group, the beneficial functioning of the market operates through an "invisible hand" that must not be impeded by the efforts or designs of those who are necessarily ignorant of its larger machinery.

Hayek insists that the unfettered operation of the free market will produce the greatest overall benefit, but he acknowledges that the impersonal functioning of the free market will result in some people suffering harm:

> I has of course to be admitted that the manner in which the benefits and burdens are apportioned by the market mechanism would in many instances have to be regarded as very unjust if it were the result of deliberate allocation to particular people. But this is not the case. Those shares are the outcome of a process the effect of which on particular people was neither intended nor foreseen by anyone when the institutions first appeared – institutions which were then permitted to continue because it was found that they improve for all or most the prospects of having their needs satisfied.
>
> *Hayek 1976, 64–65*

The market cannot be judged by "social justice" standards any more than we can complain of injustice when a tornado strikes a community. Suffering from a tornado is unfortunate but has nothing to do with social justice; the impersonal operations of the free market benefit some and harm others but like the effects of the tornado that is not injustice.

When the market results in poverty for some and riches for a few, or causes harm to many people – harms from dangerous products such as tobacco and opiates, harms to the shared environment, harms to those persuaded to spend on products of little or even negative value – that is no reason to suppose that the market needs restrictions and regulations. To the contrary, exercising market *freedom* entails being *responsible* for the results: whether riches or poverty, the market honors your free choices and yields your just deserts. Without real consequences, the neoliberals insist, there is no genuine freedom. The "freedom to fail" is part of the charm. For neoliberals, freedom and individual moral responsibility are inseparable. As Hayek (1960/2011, 69) stated, "To be free may mean freedom to starve, to make costly mistakes, or to run mortal risks." When someone lands in poverty as a result of market transactions, most think that's unfortunate; neoliberals view it as justice, confirmation of a well-functioning market, and certainly *not* a problem to be ameliorated. The free market weighs you in the balance, and you are either successful or found wanting, and there is no appeal from its verdict. As neoliberalism critic Simon Clarke notes, in neoliberalism, "Every individual has the freedom to choose the fate that will befall him or her, so the judgement of the market is a moral judgement. Hard work, foresight, initiative and enterprise will be rewarded, while the idle and lethargic will suffer their just punishment" (Clarke 2005, 55).

Efforts to "correct" the impersonal market outcomes by taking resources from the rich to aid the poor are steps down a dreadful and inexorable path toward a totalitarian system that destroys all freedom of choice: "So long as the belief in 'social justice' governs political action, this process must progressively approach nearer and nearer to a totalitarian system" (1976, 232). For neoliberalism, the state exists solely for the purpose of protecting individual liberty (including particularly the liberty to participate freely in the market) and the right of private property. Anything beyond that minimal state is an illegitimate restriction on individual freedom. Because entrepreneurs and consumers make independent and free marketplace decisions and cast their "votes" whenever they do so, the only real democracy is marketplace democracy.

In neoliberalism, all aspects of social and political life must be governed by market concerns and principles: all persons are rational economic actors or rational entrepreneurs. Rather than commitment to egalitarian principles, neoliberals extol "the equal right to inequality": the right of everyone to make their own decisions and enjoy or suffer the consequences. Everything focuses on the individual. Prime minister Margaret Thatcher, an early and passionate advocate of neoliberal policies, championed radical individualism not as policy but as indubitable fact: "There is no such thing as society. There are individual men and women, and there are families" (Thatcher 1987). As David Harvey summarizes Thatcher's crusade: "All forms of social solidarity were to be dissolved in favour of individualism, private property, personal responsibility, and family values" (2015, 23).[1] Your success and your property are entirely your own and carry no obligations to anyone. Each person is strictly an *individual* entrepreneur: The poets may say that "no man is an island," but in neoliberalism, *every* man is an island. "Ask not for whom the bell tolls," because if it does not toll for thee, then it is irrelevant noise.

Neoliberal Submission

*Neo*liberalism (both proto and contemporary) adds another key principle that distinguishes it from traditional economic liberalism: the necessity for *submission* to the operations and judgments of the market. The free market must be *protected* from those who wish to control and distort the market for their own selfish benefit (or the special benefit of their communities or families), rather than accepting the objective judgment of the market. Liberal economics places great faith in the *free market* as the optimum instrument for maximizing wealth; *neo*liberals (and their proto-neoliberal American ancestors) raise that faith to sublime heights and emphasize the necessity for *guarding* the market from the masses who would interfere with its perfect functioning.

Traditional "liberalism" – as favored by Adam Smith (1776/1993) – cherished the virtues of the free market. When the market is free, with free trade and respect for private ownership, then an "invisible hand" guides the market to provide the greatest possible overall benefit, including benefits not aimed at by those freely participating in the competitive market. In traditional economic liberalism, the competitive free market provides the greatest possible benefits, and those benefits result automatically when the market operates freely. *Neo*liberals have an even more exalted confidence in the virtues of the free competitive market, but very little confidence in the ability of most people to voluntarily forgo meddling with its operations. The competitive free market will not automatically flourish; it must be protected from interference, and the larger population must be trained – even coerced – into allowing the market to function freely for the greatest possible benefit.

The masses must learn *submission* to the operations and results of the free market. That may be accomplished by means of indoctrination (perhaps with the aid of religion); but harsher measures are justified by the ultimate market benefits. The free market will function optimally on its own, with no interference; establishing the conditions for such free hands-off functioning requires rigorous efforts and severe measures. The masses are greedy and short-sighted, they want benefits to which they are not entitled, and – like impetuous children – they want them *now*. Those who are incapable of the proper (and properly constrained) exercise of liberty must be compelled by the better people to *submit* themselves to the market judgment.

The close relation between American proto-neoliberal values and the values of contemporary neoliberalism explains why the contemporary version of neoliberalism found such a congenial home in the United States; and tracing that close relation is the major task of this book. But understanding the strength of those values in American thought requires starting with two more basic questions. First, what is the appeal of those values? Why did such values take hold in early American thought and endure through two and a half centuries? And why did those values have *general* appeal – an appeal not felt as strongly as in the United States and the United Kingdom, but still strong enough to make inroads in a wide range of cultures around the world? In short, what is the broader source of proto-neoliberal/neoliberal appeal? Second, why did those values have unusually strong and enduring – even *exceptional* – appeal in America? The first question is the subject of the next chapter, while the second question will be examined in Chapter 3.

Note

1 See also Cooper 2017, for a more extensive account of the neoliberal program of making the family and the individual responsible for all aspects of social welfare.

2

THE PSYCHOLOGY OF NEOLIBERALISM

It is obvious why the wealthy and privileged would embrace a system that guarantees not only their absolute right to their wealth but also celebrates their wisdom and transmutes their selfishness into virtue. The broader appeal of neoliberalism – extending to many who are condemned by neoliberal standards of virtue – is more difficult to understand. Neoliberalism (in both its proto and contemporary forms) taps into deep psychological needs, and examination of those powerful psychological factors helps explain both the charms of neoliberalism and the resilient cultural myths that make the United States a particularly welcoming environment for neoliberalism.

Teleological Neoliberalism

A key element of neoliberal appeal is the *purposeful* story at its core. *Teleological* explanations in terms of purposes are widely appealing: the rain falls to provide water for our crops; the hurricane moved offshore to regain strength; the plague is God's purposeful punishment for our wickedness; the kidneys exist to purify our blood. In neoliberalism, the "free market" is not merely a tool for exchange, but a purposeful force – guided by an "invisible hand" – that strives toward a positive economic goal in ways that are beyond human understanding. The complex machinations of the market are difficult to unravel, and successfully predicting market movements (unless one is blessed with inside information) is notoriously difficult. When confronted with something difficult to understand, teleological explanations – that "explain" complex phenomena in terms of comfortable and familiar *purposes* – are very appealing: whether the teleological model is the Aristotelian system of "everything seeking its proper place" or the biological explanations of a

DOI: 10.4324/9781003284680-2

benevolent purposeful deity (who fashions hands and eyes for our benefit) or the "invisible hand" that purposefully guides the free market to beneficial results.

That is not to suggest that all teleological explanations are bad; to the contrary, even when flawed they are often useful. The Aristotelian-Ptolemaic model of the universe provided a valuable pattern and sense of control for many centuries when no better explanatory model was available. The problem is that teleological explanations – in terms of purposes – are so natural and appealing (and often deeply entrenched) that they can block better explanations when those become available: the Aristotelian-Ptolemaic teleological model impeded adoption of the Copernican-Galilean model of astronomy and physics, and many still prefer the cherished "divine designer" account of biology to Darwin.

Whether humans, baboons, or chimpanzees, teleological thinking is vitally important for closely grouped social animals. Understanding the purposes of our group members is essential for our health and safety. We must distinguish a purposeful attack from an accident, mark the difference between a threat and a greeting, distinguish a sincere desire for reconciliation from a ploy to lure a target within range of attack. Is this friendly greeting from an office adversary an attempt to repair our relationship or exploit my gullibility? The same needs exist for our baboon and chimpanzee cousins. Does this powerful male wish to admire and caress my infant, or kill it (Cheney and Seyfarth 2007)? When this powerful young male selects a large stone, does he intend it for cracking nuts or as part of an aggressive challenge to my alpha status? Purposeful actors are among the most dangerous as well as the most beneficial forces in our environment, and understanding their purposes is essential for survival.

Understanding social behavior in terms of purposes is a deeply ingrained and often valuable natural tendency. Teleological explanations reveal complex patterns, organize experience, and give us a sense of control; and that is beneficial, at least until better explanations are available (in the case of the Aristotelian-Ptolemaic system, better explanations were not available for many centuries). When teleological explanations were the best we could do, we lived better with bad explanations and limited control than with a sense of disorder and helplessness.

Another advantage of teleological explanations is that – unlike mechanical explanations, such as those by Galileo and Newton and Darwin – teleological explanations are readily available. Daniel Kahneman describes the automatic and often nonconscious System 1 thinking that "operates automatically and quickly, with little or no effort and no sense of voluntary control" and distinguishes it from System 2 deliberation which "allocates attention to the effortful mental activities that demand it, including complex computations" (2011, 20–21). Jonathan Haidt characterizes System 2 deliberation as a "rider" who acts as public relations officer for the System 1 "elephant" of effective nonconscious mental processes:

> The rider acts as the spokesperson for the elephant, even though it doesn't necessarily know what the elephant is really thinking. The rider is skilled at fabricating post hoc explanations for whatever the elephant has just done, and it is good at finding reasons to justify what the elephant wants to do next.
>
> *(2012, 46)*

We not only act purposefully, but our System 2 deliberation is adept at fashioning teleological accounts of our acts in terms of socially acceptable purposes.

The Church and its Aristotelian allies waged a fierce and brutal battle, but the work of Copernicus, Kepler, Galileo, and ultimately Newton made teleological explanations of physics and astronomy obsolete. Eliminating teleological explanations in geology and biology was an even tougher challenge. As Edward J. Larson notes, the best geologists of the late-eighteenth and early-nineteenth centuries disagreed on many points, but there was one area of consensus: "For all these naturalists, from the devoutest Christians to the rankest materialists, geologic history had a beginning, a direction, and a probable end" (2004, 47). The belief that both geological and biological developments have a meaningful and purposeful direction exerts a powerful hold whether one is the "devoutest Christian" or "rankest materialist." Teleological explanations of the emergence of new species were readily available and seemed more plausible and certainly more satisfying than any explanation involving a purposeless mechanical process of natural selection. Louis Agassiz wrote to Adam Sedgwick that a divine Creator *must* have fashioned successive species according to a purposeful plan:

> This serial connection of all successive creatures is not material; taken singly these groups of species show no relation through intermediate forms genetically derived one from the other. The connection between them becomes evident only when they are considered as a whole emanating from a creative power.
>
> *quoted in Larson 2004, 43*

The details might be in dispute, but the reality – and the charm – of a creation crafted by divine purpose was not in doubt.

Promiscuous Teleology

Teleological explanations are valuable and congenial for social animals like humans. But sometimes they become too congenial, and they block superior explanations in terms of mechanical causes. Rather than evolving through natural selection, the hand was designed by a divine director to facilitate grasping objects. Diseases are not caused by toxins or viruses or bacteria but are instead God's purposeful punishment for our sins. Sexual orientations are not shaped by genes and environment but are the product of purposeful choice. The days become longer and warmer in the summer to make our crops grow. God sends rainbows to reassure us of His covenant with humans and all living things.

The English poet, John Keats, complained that science (or "natural philosophy") causes "all charms to fly":

> Clip an angel's wings,
> Conquer all mysteries by rule and line,
> Empty the haunted air, and gnomèd mine –
> Unweave a rainbow …
>
> *Lamia* 1820

Teleological explanations positing the purposeful efforts of angels and spirits and gnomes (and invisible hands) are in many ways more appealing than the mechanical explanations that replace them. They are simpler, more easily understood, and more readily available. When such "explanations" are favored over superior mechanical explanations – when God's design blocks accounts of natural selection, and explanations based on God's wrath are preferred to scientific accounts of viral infections (as many people preferred to understand the AIDS epidemic) – then teleological explanations have outlived their usefulness by impeding scientific explanations that facilitate prediction and control and improved understanding. "Promiscuous teleology" is the name psychological researchers have assigned to the powerful tendency to prefer purposive explanations even when better mechanical explanations are available. Teleological *purpose-driven* explanations are common and comfortable, and we "discover" purposeful patterns everywhere (Csibra et al. 1999; Csibra and Gergely 1998).

A strong inclination toward promiscuous teleology appears to be a human universal: every culture tested (Casler and Kelemen 2008; Kelemen 2003; Kelemen and DiYanni 2005; Mills and Frowley 2014; Schachner et al. 2017) revealed its power. The broad appeal of teleological explanations is not surprising, but the strength and persistence of promiscuous teleology is impressive. Small children favor teleological explanations and are adept at inventing them (Kelemen 2004), and the teleological tendency persists into adulthood. Adults, especially highly educated adults, often manage to resist the charms of promiscuous teleology, but the appeal of teleological explanation survives. In the face of solid systemic evidence for Darwinian evolution, many adults still prefer accounts that appeal to God's purposes (Kelemen 2012).

The tenacity of teleological explanations is discouraging, though not surprising. When university undergraduates (Kelemen and Rosset 2009) are given reflective reasoning tasks, the students choose (where appropriate) physical-causal over teleological alternatives. But under time pressure the students often favor flawed teleological explanations. Under time pressure even highly trained physical scientists fall back on convenient teleological explanations (Kelemen, Rottman, and Seston 2013). Our evolutionary ancestors thought teleologically, as do our primate cousins and our children, and so do we. Even when we know that the subject is one in which teleological explanation is inappropriate, teleological explanation remains a constant and charming temptation.

It is hardly surprising, then, that neoliberals were beguiled by the story of the invisible hand: it offers a neat and understandable teleological explanation for the complex machinations of the market. Having themselves succumbed to the powerful temptation of promiscuous teleology to explain the complex world of economic systems, they became true believer evangelists for their teleological account of market operations: an account that transformed the cold and complicated market into not only a purposeful force, but a *benevolent* purposeful force that transmutes individual greed into a wider and greater optimum benefit, and with no need for planning; to the contrary, efforts to improve the omniscient market judgement thwart the beneficent purposeful operations of the invisible hand. All that is required of the beneficiaries is humble submission to the will of the market.

The Invisible Hand

For Adam Smith, there were many instances of "the invisible hand" operating to yield results very different from the goals of the striving individuals. Maximizing economic output was just one example of a positive result that was *directed* by forces larger than the efforts of human individuals. The directing force might not be a specific deity, but instead some spiritual source guiding the world – perhaps more like an Aristotelian *inspiring* god rather than a direct interventionist Hebraic or Christian god – but still a source of positive direction. For Adam Ferguson – who strongly influenced Hayek's heavy reliance on the invisible hand – the invisible hand was clearly attached to a spiritual source. As Jessica Whyte makes clear, "Ferguson saw order as a result of providential design" (2019b, 167): the design of "an omniscient divine steward who ordered the world for our benefit" (Whyte 2019b, 168).

Given the obvious cruelty of nature, belief in a god who governs the world by a well-ordered and beneficent natural law requires strong faith. Belief in a god-directed natural law in the *absence* of a god requires super faith, or perhaps super credulity. The "invisible hand" is an article of faith – certainly not an empirically based conclusion – of neoliberal disciples. A central element of Milton Friedman's neoliberalism (Macleod 2007) is the doctrine that if all persons pursue their own economic interests, then the result will be for the benefit of all: an "invisible hand" produces larger *overall* positive results from the combination of individuals pursuing their own narrower interests. It is a charming idea, and much of its appeal comes from the paradoxical nature of the model: self-interested individuals pursuing their own narrow interests produce a general benefit for the good of all when none of the individuals were aiming at that larger goal. Indeed, it is precisely by *not* pursuing "the good of all" that the genuine larger good is produced, while policies *aimed* at more general benefits fail to secure those benefits (and are more likely to shrink than expand the overall good). Individual selfishness is transformed by the invisible hand into large-scale virtue, while the proposed projects of those who aim at producing economic benefits for all – projects launched with virtuous and generous intent – cause great harm. By the good offices of the invisible hand, you can selfishly eat your cake and at the same time produce a bigger cake for the enjoyment of all.

Belief in a Just World

Promiscuous teleology is part of the explanation for the appeal of neoliberalism. Another part of that explanation involves a second widespread psychological phenomenon that meshes with the neoliberalism purposeful story: the deep but generally nonconscious Belief in a Just World (BJW). Nonconscious BJW is powerful, pervasive, and well-established by a body of psychological research spanning several decades and encompassing dozens of studies (Furnham 2003; Hafer and Bègue 2005). This deep belief is both common and cross-cultural, though it is stronger in some cultures than others. Adrian Furnham gives a clear statement of the basic BJW: "The BJW asserts that, quite justly, good things tend to happen to good people and bad things to bad people despite the fact that this is patently not the case" (2003, 795).

BJW gives us a sense of a well-ordered world and thus encourages our positive efforts:

> Individuals have a need to believe that they live in a world where people generally get what they deserve. The belief that the world is just enables the individual to confront his physical and social environments as though they were stable and orderly. Without such a belief it would be difficult for the individual to commit himself to the pursuit of long range goals or even to the socially regulated behaviour of day to day life .... Since the belief that the world is just serves such an important adaptive function for the individual, people are very reluctant to give up this belief, and they can be greatly troubled if they encounter evidence that suggests that the world is not really just or orderly after all.
>
> *Lerner and Miller 1978, 1031*

A key principle of neoliberalism is that the free market is the optimum method of giving everyone their *just deserts*. Guided by the invisible hand, the free-market rewards and punishes in accordance with *objective* and decisive principles of justice. The disturbing *appearance* of injustice – some enjoy luxuries while others suffer hardship – is explained away, and the comforting BJW is protected.

Innocent victims threaten our comfortable BJW, and the most convenient way of preserving that belief is by changing the status of the victims from innocent to guilty. The case of rape victims is the most obvious and extensively studied example of this phenomenon. Rape is a brutal, demeaning, and trauma-producing crime; in a just world, no innocent person would be subjected to such a horrific fate. Faced with this challenge, nonconscious BJW portrays rape victims as not quite so innocent: they dressed provocatively; they were "loose" women; they did something to put themselves in that situation; they "led him on" or were "asking for it." Harsh cross-examinations of rape victims are notoriously common and often effective: jurors – eager to preserve their BJW – are already inclined to see the victim as other than innocent.

Rape victims were provocative, the poor are lazy, refugees lack motivation. The stronger the BJW, the greater the likelihood of blaming victims for their misfortune (Furnham and Gunter 1984; Dalbert and Yamauchi 1994; Harper and Manasse1992; Montada 1998; Wagstaff 1983). We blame innocent victims and innocent victims – such as abused children – often blame themselves rather than face an unjust world (Lerner 1980, 123–125). BJW transforms innocent victims into guilty villains who get what they deserve.

The history of philosophy is rich with desperate efforts to prop up BJW. As Bernard Williams notes, the belief that the world is ethically well-ordered and just – the belief that justice is built into the *structure* of the world – has had a powerful influence on the history of philosophical thought: "Plato, Aristotle, Kant, Hegel are all on the same side, all believing in one way or another that the universe or history or the structure of human reason can, when properly understood, yield a pattern that makes sense of human life and human aspirations" (1993, 163). Plato insisted that a just man will invariably experience a better life than an unjust; Aristotle, that a morally good life is the most likely path to genuine flourishing; Kant, that the world *must* be such that we can always fulfill our moral obligations. Williams argues that Kant's rationalistic moral philosophy offers an "equal capacity" justification of moral responsibility and a just world:

> The capacity for moral agency is supposedly present to any rational agent whatsoever, to anyone for whom the question can even present itself. The successful moral life, removed from considerations of birth, lucky upbringing, or indeed of the incomprehensible Grace of a non-Pelagian God, is presented as a career open not merely to the talents, but to a talent which all rational beings necessarily possess in the same degree. Such a conception has an ultimate form of justice at its heart, and that

> is its allure. Kantianism is only superficially repulsive – despite appearances, it offers an inducement, solace to a sense of the world's unfairness.
>
> *(1981, 21)*

"Solace to a sense of the world's unfairness" and a prop for BJW is purchased at a steep price: exacerbation of the world's unfairness, together with a distorted view of human reason.

Paul of Tarsus believed in a just world: "Be not deceived; God is not mocked: for whatsoever a man soweth, that shall he also reap" (Galatians 6:7 KJV). The Hindu tradition teaches the same principle: "As a man himself sows, so he himself reaps; no man inherits the good or evil act of another man. The fruit is of the same quality as the action" (Mahabharata, xii.291.22). Sharon Salzberg writes best-selling books on self-improvement and teaches Buddhist meditation, and she has no doubt that our world is just: "Things don't just happen in this world of arising and passing away. We don't live in some kind of crazy, accidental universe. Things happen according to certain laws, laws of nature. Laws such as the law of karma, which teaches us that as a certain seed gets planted, so will that fruit be" (Salzberg 2010). In contrast, Jesus of Nazareth knew that there are many who "reap where they did not sow," and that those who do the hard work of sowing often are deprived of benefits by those who practice usury or other exploitative methods (Matt. 25: 24–29 KJV). Like all Jews, he was painfully aware that in contests between virtue and Roman might, virtue had suffered a sad string of defeats.

In the gospel accounts, Jesus rejects the belief that our world is just. In contrast, orthodox Christianity – with its commitment to an *omnipotent* and omniscient God who is also *just* – has long struggled with the problem of evil: How can this omnipotent, just and all-knowing God allow the suffering of innocent infants? In his debate with Julian, Augustine argued that the suffering of children is *proof* of God's justice: the children are *not* innocent victims but are corrupted by original sin and their suffering is justly deserved. The suffering of children is conclusive evidence of their vile sinful nature because we know God is just and a just God would never allow *innocents* to undergo such suffering. Julian had claimed that "At the beginning of life, human nature is adorned with the gift of innocence." Challenging Julian, Augustine argued that because infants suffer, they *must* be sinful and thus justly deserve their suffering:

> If he contracted no evil from his origin, he would never be born with even bodily faults. For God, who is the creator of souls, is also the creator of bodies, and He would never undeservedly inflict faults on human nature in its very creation. . . . God forbid we say this is done without its being deserved.
>
> *(1957, 118)*

The Neoliberal Just World

Maintaining BJW may require the positing of additional life cycles, or perhaps an afterlife of torture or bliss, or even a commitment to the evil nature of infants – but BJW must be protected, at all costs. Like God, the ways of the free market are beyond our understanding; but in both cases, we know that the judgments are *just*: everyone gets what they objectively and justly deserve through the operations of the free market, and the *appearance* of injustice (which threatens our comfortable BJW) is explained away by the just but inscrutable purposeful operations of the free market. And, surely it *is* just. Nathanael Chipman, a proto-neoliberal Continental Army officer who later became a Senator, explains why the operations of the free market are just, and why *interference* in market judgments – by taking resources from the wealthy (who justly deserve their wealth) to aid the poor (who justly deserve their poverty) – is a double wrong:

> Riches are the fruit of industry. Honor the fruit of merit. Both ought, as to their continuance, and the influence which attends them, to be left to the conduct of the possessor. If a man, who, by industry and economy, has acquired riches, become indolent, or profligate, let him sink into poverty. Let those who are still industrious and economical, succeed to his enjoyments, as to their just reward. . . . To exclude the meritorious from riches and honors, and to perpetuate either to the undeserving, are equally injurious to the rights of man in society. In both it is to counteract the laws of nature, which have, by the connection of cause and effect, annexed the proper rewards and punishments to the actions of men. Wealth, or at least, a competency, is the reward, provided by the laws of nature, for prudent industry; want, the punishment of idleness and profligacy.
>
> *Chipman 1793*

Hayek recognized that the belief in a "just world" – in which people are rewarded or punished based on their own efforts and (self-made) abilities – paved the way for acceptance of the belief that the results of the market are just, and both rich and poor are receiving their just rewards. Hayek himself doubted that belief in a just economic world can sustain devotion to the free market. He preferred that commitment to the free market be based on faith that the market provides the greatest overall material benefit and that it maximizes individual freedom, but he acknowledged that belief in the *justice* of the market has been a powerful motive behind the popularity of the free-market ideology in the United States:

> It is probably a misfortune that, especially in the USA, popular writers like Samuel Smiles and Horatio Alger, and later the sociologist W.G.

> Sumner, have defended free enterprise on the ground that it regularly rewards the deserving, and it bodes ill for the future of the market order that this seems to have become the only defence of it which is understood by the general public. That it has largely become the basis of the self-esteem of the businessman often gives him an air of self-righteousness, which does not make him more popular.
>
> *Hayek 1976, 237–238*

Selfishness is usually considered a vice, and the wealthy are often selfish and brutally indifferent to the suffering of the less fortunate (Piff 2010; Wang and Murnighan 2014). But how – in a just world – can those poor in virtue be rich in possessions? Why do the wicked prosper? In the neoliberal world, the wealthy prosper because they *earn* their wealth by their efforts and their superior talents, and so they justly deserve the benefits (besides, they are the "job creators"); while the poor are lazy and justly deserve their suffering. But above all, the wise market is the sole arbiter of justice and the only authority for determining just economic deserts. The market alone combines the full range and depth of knowledge that transcends any limited source of judgment, and there is no appeal from the verdict of the free market. What appears – from a limited perspective – to be selfish behavior is actually exercise of virtue, because it creates more wealth for the whole society: the rising economic tide raises all – or many – boats, even if some are raised much higher than others.

During the Gilded Age, it was difficult to call the wealthy virtuous: they indulged in conspicuous consumption while many of those who did the hard work and made possible their fortunes went hungry. The wealthy came up with a different justification, equally implausible: social Darwinism. Those who come out on top are clearly superior in this fiercely competitive "survival of the fittest." They must prosper because only through the flourishing of the successful best people (and the demise of the economic losers) will society advance. But whether neoliberalism or social Darwinism, there is a powerful need to justify the claim that even the most obviously egregious behavior by the wealthy *must* in some way be virtuous: both the wealthy and the poor want to believe in a just world. Jessica Whyte (2019a, 231) emphasizes that neoliberalism was not just an economic doctrine, but also a system of ethical principles and doctrines that were contrived to provide moral justification for neoliberalism. BJW was fundamental to those efforts.

We want to preserve our BJW, we especially want to believe that our own acts are just, and we must convince ourselves that our own prosperity and privileges are the justly deserved reward of our noble natures and virtuous behavior. For many of the world's greedy and unscrupulous wealthy, that is a task almost as daunting as proving that suffering children are fundamentally evil. The task is made easier when it is framed in a charming *story*: a story that "explains" virtuous selfishness through the part it plays in a larger purposeful narrative which – like the diligent tortoise's triumph over the swift but lethargic hare – has a surprising twist and an uplifting moral. The story of the invisible hand is the perfect fit. The invisible hand doesn't just operate; rather (as Adam Smith says) we are "led by the invisible hand." The invisible hand *purposefully guides* us, it *leads* us to prosperity and freedom and justice. Neoliberalism tells a comfortable teleological tale with a happy ending.

3

AMERICAN NEOLIBERALISM

In the European tradition, differences in wealth and privilege were justified by God's will: the king and his nobles were God's anointed. But the new US had no nobility, no king; it was a country in which "all men are created equal," and in which the people would rule themselves. The elite proclaimed a message of freedom and equality, though in private they made sure that the elite would still rule and would retain their disproportionate wealth against any encroachment by the masses. They needed a new justification for their power and wealth, one that did not depend on God's judgment. The new justification was based on market meritocracy: wealth indicates that you are virtuous and industrious; poor, you are indolent and getting what you justly deserve. One's level of wealth and property was the objective judge of worth: only those with substantial property were allowed to vote, and eligibility for office required even more property. Contemporary neoliberalism built on what was already present as a legacy of the Founding Fathers.

Neoliberalism has obvious charms for the wealthy, but it also appeals to Americans who are far from wealthy: many who suffer economic and social harm from the neoliberal system are among its passionate defenders. The appeal of neoliberalism runs far beyond what can be accounted for by narrow self-interest. Why did neoliberalism take root in the United States, among both the extremely wealthy as well as the much greater number of people who live in poverty or are balanced precariously on the edge of poverty – where a lost job or a serious illness could push them over the edge? Understanding the factors that make neoliberalism popular in the United States requires deeper examination of forces that shaped the American culture.

DOI: 10.4324/9781003284680-3

The Founding Fathers and Proto-Neoliberalism

The roots of US neoliberalism run deep – all the way down to the American Revolution and the framing of the US constitution. Many of the basic neoliberal values were powerfully present among the American elite of the Revolutionary period: in particular, the merits of the free market, political control by a small elite class, the supreme value of private property, a special understanding of "freedom," the virtue of individual personal responsibility – and even a version of the neoliberal position on colonialism, insisting on the rights of "advanced" civilizations to claim and use any resources not being "properly exploited" by "backwards" (in this case, indigenous American) peoples.

Jessica Whyte constructs a rigorous and insightful analysis of neoliberalism, and she emphasizes the importance of political and ethical arguments in the triumph of neoliberalism:

> We cannot understand the neoliberal victory if we view it only in economic terms. The success of neoliberalism was not predicated merely on its arguments for the superior efficiency of markets, or its challenges to the economics of socialist planning. Rather, neoliberals pioneered a series of political arguments about the dangers of wealth redistribution, interference with the market and mass participation in politics, especially in the post-colony, that helped to legitimise austerity and the crushing of Third Worldist demands for global wealth redistribution.
>
> *(2019a, 231)*

It is striking how well Whyte's analysis – with just a few words changed – applies to the program of the American Founding Fathers in taking control for the wealthy and keeping the poor powerless. To paraphrase Whyte: The Founding Fathers pioneered a series of political arguments about the dangers of wealth redistribution, interference with the market and mass participation in politics (especially for the poor and less educated), arguments that legitimized austerity and the crushing of rural farmers' demands for a greater share of the wealth. It is not surprising that contemporary neoliberalism found a good home in the United States: the foundations of that comfortable home had been laid by the proto-neoliberal Founding Fathers who framed the US constitution.

Freedom, Democracy, and the Founding Fathers

Whyte's analysis of the success of the neoliberalism "political arguments" emphasizes the importance of a distinctive value framework and value vocabulary that was essential to the spread of neoliberalism. A vital element of that values package was a special definition of "freedom" – meaning essentially market freedom and the freedom of unrestricted private property ownership. The founders – like contemporary neoliberals – exploited the strong positive regard for human freedom to promote a special restricted account of freedom as "genuine freedom." The difference between the ordinary meaning of freedom and the version promoted by neoliberals as well as by the Founding Fathers is made brutally clear when one considers that for the Founding Fathers the "freedom" of slave owners to be secure in their human "property" took precedence over any "freedom" that was denied to those in bondage. Above all, property rights *must* be protected, and the right of *free possession of property* was far more important than any concern about freedom from slavery. Furthermore, it was generally assumed by the framers of the constitution – slave owners as well as abolitionists – that any abolition of slavery would require compensating the slave owners for the loss of their property (compensating slaves for the loss of their labor and their freedom was never considered). The right of slaves to freedom was insignificant when compared to the sublime right of free possession of property.

Contemporary neoliberals make their views palatable by taking advantage of the deep appeal of the idea of freedom: trumpeting their love of *freedom for all* while narrowing freedom to the freedom of the marketplace, the freedom of absolute protection of property, the freedom to suffer the just deserts of poverty; but *not* the freedom of self-government (which is the privilege of the elite). The proto-neoliberal Founding Fathers used the same trick, making the country a favorable environment for the later triumph of neoliberalism and its glorification of marketplace "freedom." But the Founding Fathers added another trick that has long been a valuable all-purpose tool in the political toolbox: hypocritical deceit. For public consumption, the framers of the constitution extolled the virtues of a country of free and equal citizens with a government by the people and for the people: ring the liberty bell and celebrate democracy. But in their secret sessions, they constructed a constitution that would effectively block the democracy they despised and preserve power exclusively for the wealthy elite: the elite *best people* as marked by the blessings of the market are the only ones fit to govern.

The Founding Fathers preached equality and democracy; they promoted elitism, oligarchy, and the fundamental rights of property (including property in slaves). The sad reality – difficult to confront for a country that celebrates the Founding Fathers as paragons of virtue, intellect, public-spiritedness, and integrity – is that the Founding Fathers were lying self-interested hypocrites. It's bad enough to pull Robert E. Lee from his pedestal and reveal him as a cruel slave master who treated his slaves harshly and inflicted horrific torture on those who sought freedom. It is even harder to acknowledge that Christopher Columbus was a genocidal monster who burned captives for sadistic celebrations. But it is still more disturbing to turn a harsh light on the Father of the Country – exposing his devotion to slavery, his aversion to democracy, his profound elitism, his callous disdain for the suffering of the poor farmers who had fought for independence, and his two-faced promotion of democracy to the masses while joining his wealthy friends at the constitutional convention to block democracy.

The great American myth is that the United States was founded as a democracy – as a unique country that (in the stirring words of Abraham Lincoln) established a government "of the people, by the people, for the people)" and if the United States failed, then that form of government would "perish from the earth." But the Founding Fathers never intended to establish a democracy. To the contrary, their major concern was to find a way to keep the people under control and prevent the "masses" from gaining governmental power and interfering in the sacred free market. Whether proto or contemporary neoliberals, democracy was considered a danger; as David Harvey notes, "neoliberal theorists are . . . profoundly suspicious of democracy" (2005, 66). The founders' primary goal was to protect property rights, and their great fear was that a democracy would emerge in which the people would demand a more equitable distribution of property. But those were values the proto-neoliberal Founding Fathers espoused in private. For public consumption – and to draw the support of the masses they despised – they relied on inspiring but empty words: "We hold these truths to be self-evident, that all men are created equal, that they are endowed by their Creator with certain unalienable Rights, and among these are Life, Liberty, and pursuit of Happiness." That the words were written by a slave holder – and that five of the first six US presidents were slave holders – is clear evidence that such noble principles served as window dressing, never intended as reality or even aspiration. Rather than believing that "all men are created equal," they regarded it as obvious that some men (women were hardly worthy of mention) were far superior to others, and that slaves could not conceivably be counted as equals. The superior men were those who held land and wealth, and they were the only persons who could be trusted with governmental power. Rather than endeavoring to create a country run "by the people and for the people," the main goal was to prevent the people from gaining power and making claims on the wealth and property of their superiors.

When struggling to raise an army to fight for independence, the emphasis was on equality and democracy; when writing a constitution, the concern was making sure that the masses of people with little or no property could never exercise effective control of the government, for fear that they would demand that the property of the wealthy be more evenly distributed. When soldiers were needed to fight the British, democracy and equality were cherished principles; when the battles were won, it was essential that the "best people" – "the rich and well born," as Alexander Hamilton described them – remain in power, and that the poor and lowly learn to accept the ruling judgments of the elite and submit themselves to the justice of the free market. The flowery words of the declaration of independence were for public consumption; when speaking in private to their fellow superior beings – as they spoke, in rigorous secrecy, during the constitutional convention – they sang a very different tune. They favored substantial property ownership as a condition for voting, and even stronger standards for holding office, and their greatest value was the protection of property: property they feared would be threatened by the rise of democracy. Poor people could die fighting for independence, but they could not be trusted with the government of their country; above all, they could not be trusted to protect the wealth of the elite and the independence of the free market.

Gouverneur Morris – born to great wealth and privilege at his family's manor near New York City – expressed the consensus of the constitutional convention: "the ignorant and the dependent can be as little trusted with the public interest" as small children (quoted in Klarman 2016, 178). John Dickinson (Convention delegate from Delaware) agreed, insisting that only those with substantial property should be allowed to vote, as a "necessary defense against the dangerous influence of those multitudes without property and without principle" (quoted in Klarman 2016, 179). As Michael J. Klarman notes, Benjamin Franklin was one of the few delegates who opposed property requirements for voting and holding office, noting that "some of the greatest rogues he was ever acquainted with were the richest rogues" (2016, 179). But that was a view that the rich rogues who framed the US constitution did not embrace. Charles Pinckney proposed property qualifications that would make less than 1% of the population eligible for membership in Congress (Klarman 2016, 181). Klarman bluntly describes the actual attitude of the framers of the constitution toward democracy:

> Behind the closed doors of the Philadelphia convention, the delegates outdid one another in the contempt they expressed for democracy. Gerry called democracy "the worst . . . of all political evils." Sherman declared that the people "should have as little to do as may be about the government. They want [i.e., lack] information and are constantly liable to be misled." Hamilton observed that . . . "The people are turbulent and changing; they seldom judge or determine right." . . . Virtually all the delegates ... could agree upon the proposition that ordinary citizens ought not to have too great a role in governmental affairs.
>
> *(2016, 244)*

The primary goal of government must be to protect private property, and the great danger to private property is to be found (as Virginia delegate Edmund Randolph warned) "in the turbulence and follies of democracy" (quoted in Klarman 2016, 245). The Founding Fathers set up a system that protects wealth and prevents democracy, and – as Alberto Alesina and Edward L. Glaeser note – they built a system that endures to this day:

> Conservative predominance within the United States was associated with a nonproportional electoral system, a presidential system, a powerful system of checks and balances enforced by the Senate (a millionaire's club until the early twentieth century), and a powerful Supreme Court with a mission to defend private property. All of these political institutions were heavily influenced by the desire to limit the amount of redistribution that the poor could impose on the rich.
>
> *(2004, 219)*

The effort to prevent democratic self-government was not an aberration, but a process that the ruling elite have pursued from the Revolution to the present. As Annelien de Dijn notes, in the early 19th century the opposition to democracy dominated: "American political movements rejected the revolutionary definition of freedom as democratic self-government, arguing instead that freedom was the preservation of personal security and the protection of individual rights – notably property rights" (2020, 266). The abolitionist fervor and Reconstruction policies created a brief exceptional period when support for American democracy was relatively strong and suffrage somewhat expanded, but Reconstruction soon gave way to the oppressive policies and practices of the Jim Crow era, and advances toward democracy were brutally reversed. The "Gilded Age" (from 1870 to 1900) was a period in which democratic policies were under concerted attack:

> The Gilded Age was characterized by a widespread push to make voting harder not just for blacks but also for poor whites and immigrants in the crowded cities of the North. An increasing number of states in the North and West introduced literacy requirements. In addition, residency requirements were made more onerous, and paupers who had received public aid were excluded from voting. . . . Such measures were often presented as necessary to combat voter fraud.
>
> *De Dijn 2020, 307*

In the first half of the 20th century, the women's suffrage movement and FDR's New Deal promoted democratic ideals, but after 1945, the Cold War and anti-communism were powerful tools for defeating efforts by workers and minorities and the poor for a voice in government – and also provided a special opportunity for the popularizing of Hayek's anti-socialist neoliberalism. Democracy is seen – as the Founders also viewed it – as a threat to liberty and individual rights, especially the pre-eminent rights related to private property.

Failed Struggles against Proto-Neoliberalism

The Fugitive Slave Clause – requiring the authorities in all states to assist in returning escaped slaves to their "rightful owners" – was passed by the constitutional convention without a single dissenting vote, and apparently without objection. There were delegates who disliked slavery, but slaves were property, and the importance of preserving property rights took precedence over any concerns about the wrongness of slavery.

Another powerful mark of the supreme importance of private property can be found in two important events in the years following the American Revolution: Shays' Rebellion and the Whiskey Rebellion. Together they made clear both the deep commitment of the elite to private property and the supreme rights of creditors as well as their lack of concern for the welfare of the less affluent farmers and workers. If the free market results in suffering for the poor, that is the verdict of the market to which the unfortunate should and must submit – compelled by overwhelming force, if necessary.

Daniel Shays joined the Continental army at the beginning of hostilities and served courageously from 1775 to 1780. He was promoted to sergeant for his bravery at the Battle of Lexington, served under Ethan Allen in the capture of Fort Ticonderoga, fought in the Battle of Saratoga, and stormed Stony Point under General "Mad Anthony" Wayne. He was awarded a ceremonial sword in honor of his courage at Saratoga (a sword he later sold to help pay his debts). Shays and the other farmers who joined "Shays' Rebellion" were not "sunshine patriots." They had fought in the Revolution, suffered severe hardships, and been paid with promises rather than cash.

The debts that had been incurred by the new government (much of it owed to wealthy Boston merchants) *must* be paid: not honoring the demands of sacred property was unthinkable. Taxes were passed which the rural farmers could not pay. Poll taxes – a set tax on each individual, rich or poor – was the main form of taxation. The tax was easily paid by wealthy Boston merchants, but it cost small farmers one-third of their annual income. Because gold and silver coins were in short supply – most of it was taken for use in trade with Europe – trade among the rural settlers was primarily by barter. But the high regressive taxes could not be paid by barter: gold and silver coins, which could not be obtained, were required. Several times the farmers petitioned for help, requesting that the state issue paper money that the farmers (in the absence of gold and silver) could use to pay their taxes and debts, and asking for tax relief; their requests were ignored by the Boston patricians who ran the state government, and who "blamed farmers for squandering their money in taverns and on European imports" (Klarman 2016, 90).

Many of the farmers had belonged to the state militias, where their low wages were paid in scrip – essentially, promissory notes that someday the states might manage to pay. After years of no payment, there was little reason to suppose the scrip would ever be paid off, and its value dropped to almost nothing. Wealthy speculators (or their agents) went around to desperately poor veterans buying up scrip for a fraction of its face value. Because the speculators had powerful friends in government, they convinced the legislature to pay off the scrip at full face value. "As much as 90 percent of government securities ultimately fell into the hands of speculators, who had the financial resources to be patient in holding onto them and the political clout necessary to pressure governments to redeem them at face value" (Klarman 2016, 82). A large share of the onerous taxes levied on small farmers and veterans went to pay off the speculators who had bought up the scrip of the veterans – speculators who had lived very comfortably during the War for Independence while the soldiers suffered, and who now were getting rich off the scrip they had bought from the veterans for a pittance. Farms were foreclosed and auctioned off for about a third of their value: not enough money to pay what was owed on the purchase of the farm, nor the farmer's taxes; so, the impoverished farmers were sent to debtors' prison (added to their debts were the high court costs involved in declaring them guilty of the indebtedness they could not pay). And to rub salt in the wound, they were condemned as wasteful, demanding luxuries and rum, and indolent. High property requirements for suffrage blocked many veterans from voting in the nation for whose independence they had fought and bled. Those were the circumstances leading to Shays' Rebellion in 1786 when desperate farmers in Western Massachusetts closed courthouses to stop the foreclosures on farms. The rebellion was crushed, and many of those who took part were condemned to death. Most received a pardon, but two were hanged.

A similar event occurred a few years later, following the constitutional convention. The convention decided that all US debts must be honored in full – including the scrip and bonds issued to soldiers in the Continental Army. Because most people (including the veterans) did not believe the scrip would ever be redeemed by real money, the bonds and scrip had lost almost all its value. Again, wealthy speculators swooped in and bought the scrip from veterans and the small manufacturers who had supplied the new country and then persuaded the framers of the constitution to redeem their holdings at full face value. Some who bought the bonds were "trading with inside information" (Klarman 2016, 384): the work of the constitutional convention was strictly secret, and so the framers of the constitution knew that the government would redeem the bonds and scrip at face value while most people still regarded them as almost worthless. Heavy state taxes were required to pay off the bonds and scrip now held by a small group of wealthy speculators; in Pennsylvania, one of the main sources of tax revenue selected by the legislature was a tax on whiskey, the major cash crop of the small farmers – almost the only product they could sell in Philadelphia for cash. Once again farms were being foreclosed and small farmers – including many veterans – were driven into poverty.

The Whiskey Rebellion – which peaked in 1794 – attempted to block collection of the tax and stop foreclosures. A federal army of almost thirteen thousand marched to western Pennsylvania and routed the small bands of rebels.

The wealthy American elite blamed farmers for wasting their money and being lazy – the market had weighed them in the balance and found them wanting. President George Washington showed little concern for the plight of the western Massachusetts and western Pennsylvania farmers who had fought valiantly in the Revolutionary War. He insisted they should be put down with whatever violence necessary. To give Washington his due, he did pardon some of the Whiskey Rebellion farmers: a decision that angered his friend Alexander Hamilton, who wanted to hang them all as traitors. The veterans who lost their farms and were thrown into debtors' prison were suffering the just deserts of their "idleness and sloth," and providing relief would encourage their vices and discourage personal responsibility and hard work, and thriftiness. This claim – the lazy poor justly deserve their poverty – has been made for two centuries in the United States, with contemporary neoliberal economists and legislators insisting that the reason for poverty and bankruptcy is the "lack of personal responsibility" of those who declare bankruptcy.

Personal Responsibility

In "The Past, Present, and Future of Bankruptcy Law in America," Todd J. Zywicki argues that in the United States an important "influence on the bankruptcy process is the tradition of prodebtor, populist, and progressive ideology in American politics" (2003, 2023). Perhaps there was a brief period of "progressive ideology" in the New Deal after the capitalist system crashed during the Great Depression; but the American tradition – from the Founders and the Framers through Ronald Reagan and into the present – has been the opposite of a populist and progressive ideology, instead enshrining the rights of property, celebrating "rugged individualism" and "self-made men," and condemning the poor as lazy moral failures who brought their justly deserved suffering on themselves.

Zywicki celebrates the oppressive "Bankruptcy Reform Act of 2002" – which provided enormous benefits for creditors and made the plight of those who were forced to declare bankruptcy much more difficult – as a triumph of the "personal responsibility" political ideology:

> The personal responsibility ideology sees consumer bankruptcy as primarily a moral issue, rather than an economic issue. To be sure, personal-responsibility and law-and-economics arguments often reinforce one another, as much of the personal-responsibility rhetoric stresses the injustice of forcing responsible consumers to subsidize the recklessness of profligate borrowers. But the distinction is deeper than just

> economics: soaring consumer-bankruptcy filing rates viewed as a crisis of the American soul, rather than a mere matter of economic policy. Put simply, there is no economic explanation for the upsurge in individual bankruptcy filings in the late 1990s, an era of unprecedented prosperity, low interest rates, low unemployment rates, and soaring levels of individual wealth. Given the anomaly of economic prosperity combined with the staggering rise in bankruptcy filings, many have concluded that the problem is social and spiritual rather than economic.
>
> *(2003, 2026)*

To paraphrase Shakespeare, the fault is not in our neoliberal economic system, but in ourselves, that we are indolent and depraved.

Zywicki's argument is based on a set of "half-truths" – claims that are literally true but omit information that would place those "truths" in a very different light. It is "half-true" that the late 1990s was "an era of unprecedented prosperity, low-interest rates, low unemployment rates, and soaring levels of individual wealth" (2003, 2026). In fact, interest rates for a 30-year mortgage were between 7% and 8% (more than double the current rate). And while it was certainly an era of prosperity for the very wealthy – for the top 10%, and especially the top 1%, income and wealth soared – it was not prosperous for most people. The wages of middle-wage workers were stagnant, and wages declined for low-wage workers. A study by the Economic Policy Institute found that after adjusting for inflation, wages in 1995 were nearly 3% lower than they were in 1989 (Bivens et al. 2014). There were indeed "soaring levels of individual wealth" for the few, but the middle and lower classes were not among those whose wealth soared.

Because the 1990s was "an era of unprecedented prosperity, low-interest rates, low unemployment rates, and soaring levels of individual wealth," Zywicki concludes that the increase in bankruptcies must be due to causes that are "social and spiritual, rather than economic;" that is, those individuals declaring bankruptcy must be social and spiritual reprobates. But it is obvious – except to Zywicki – that there were other factors involved in bankruptcies, and bankruptcies are not due to "social and spiritual" depravity. The failure of savings and loan associations (resulting from the reckless *deregulation* championed by neoliberals) played a part in the desperate circumstances of many middle-class savers. But a much more important factor was the occurrence of health crises. Cancer rates were increasing (often due to industrial toxins at the workplace and in the atmosphere) and the cost of cancer treatments – and other medical treatments – was increasing at a very rapid rate (well above inflation, and much more rapidly than the wages of most people). Insurance policies often covered only a fraction of medical costs. Most people who declared bankruptcy reported the costs of medical treatment (and often the loss of work due to illness) as major factors driving them into bankruptcy.

Another factor that Zywicki neglects was the intense push by retailers and credit card companies to hook consumers into high levels of indebtedness. Credit card offers constantly arrived in the mail, and credit card companies set up booths on campus and offered special gifts – a t-shirt, a water bottle, a travel coffee cup – to students who accepted a credit card. The "initial interest rate" was often low; after a few months – as the fine print noted – the rate increased substantially; and if you were late with a payment, the interest rate soared. Rather than the "low interest rates" celebrated by Zywicki, the average credit card rate was approximately 15%, and many were paying ruinous rates of 24% (not including late fees and other fees) or even higher. As Susanne Soederberg notes: "this expansion of credit took place alongside the ongoing dismantling of the social welfare state and the disappearance of secure, high-wage jobs in the productive realm, producing a social reality that dragged poorer workers into a growing reliance on private financing (e.g., credit cards) to augment or replace not only their social wages and subsistence needs, but also essential welfare services" (Soederberg 2013, 501). Retailers soon learned that they could make more money on interest than on their sales, and they offered "special deals" to those who opened a credit account, and special offers to delay paying for your purchase (while the interest accumulated). The interest rates were high, and consumers opening an account to get the "special discount" didn't always pay attention to the details; and again, a late payment sent the interest rate much higher. The powerful and widespread push to hook consumers into high-interest debts – debts that continued to increase, as consumers were encouraged to pay the minimum on their high-interest credit card accounts – were a key factor in the increase in bankruptcies. Perhaps the individuals were at fault for getting hooked into a spiral of debt at high-interest rates, but Zywicki should note the beam in the greedy eyes of the creditors before condemning the speck in the myopic eyes of the debtors.

Zywicki treats the personal responsibility ideology as a wonderful innovation of the Reagan revolution, and certainly the "Reagan Revolution" strengthened and solidified that ideology in the American political system; but the basic ideas were being celebrated behind closed doors – not for public consumption – in Philadelphia among the framers of the constitution, and they have played a dominant role in American political policy ever since. Zywicki praises the public-spirited statesmen in Congress who passed the bankruptcy reform act, and insists (2003, 2032) that the massive campaign contributions and lobbying efforts of the consumer credit industry had almost no influence on their selfless devotion to principle:

> much of Congress's interest in consumer-bankruptcy reform is rooted in values-based concerns over personal and financial responsibility. Personal bankruptcy is part of a larger set of concerns over the moral character of the nation, its leaders, and the negative impact of rampant

> breaking of one's financial promises on reliability, trust, and reciprocity in other aspects of life.
>
> *(2003, 2027)*

Members of Congress were not protecting the credit card companies that fund their political campaigns; they were protecting the moral fiber of the nation.

This is a clear echo of the wealthy patricians of Boston, whose dedication to protecting the integrity of their property enabled them to stand firm against the demands of the "indolent" western Massachusetts farmers – the veterans who fought for independence – whose farms were being foreclosed to pay off the wealthy speculators who had cornered the market on scrip. When contemporary neoliberals celebrate "personal responsibility" and denigrate those who face economic ruin – while congratulating themselves on their outstanding merits – they are not doing anything original: it has been a favorite theme of the American elite for well over two centuries. The fundamental doctrines of neoliberal elitism – including sacred property, personal responsibility, meritocracy, and the justice of the market – are as American as apple pie and older than baseball.

The United States was a proto-neoliberal country long before Hayek was born. It not only practiced the basic principles of neoliberalism but also proclaimed similar "freedom" virtues: basically, the freedom to control property, even if that property was human; not the freedom of opportunity or genuine choice or self-government. At best, the "freedom" of perfect submission, celebrated by neoliberalism. "Market freedom" is the basic freedom, without limits or restrictions. If speculators made shrewd decisions buying up soldiers' scrip, tough luck for the veterans. If they did so with insider information and special legislative influence, that was just good capitalist business: affirmed as virtuous by their economic success in the market, the only standard that counts.

The Founding Fathers proclaimed noble democratic principles of liberty and equality, while in practice they entrenched government by the wealthy and opposed democracy as government by those unfit to govern who might challenge the inequitable division of wealth. They publicly praised the principle that "all men are endowed by their Creator" with the right to liberty while writing into the constitution the property rights of slave-holders to have their escaped "property" returned to them. They preached equality and unity while practicing a devotion to radical individualism and justly deserved inequality.

The Virtuous Wealthy

The Founding Fathers wanted freedom from control by England, but the freedom they were most eager to maintain and protect was the freedom of private property and the *freedom* to compete in the free market, with each person bearing total responsibility for the outcome. The proto-neoliberal freedom of the Revolutionary period – with its praise of selfish individualism, glorification of property and wealth, and scorn for the poor – is a common theme in American thought, from the colonial era to the present. Russell Conwell was a famous 19th-century American orator – or "inspirational speaker," as he would now be described. His most famous speech, delivered hundreds of times, was "Acres of Diamonds." It celebrated the virtues of the rich and condemned the vices of the poor:

> I say that you ought to get rich, and it is your duty to get rich. . . . Let me say here clearly, ninety-eight out of one hundred of the rich men of America are honest. That is why they are rich. That is why they are trusted with money. That is why they carry on great enterprises and find plenty of people to work with them. It is because they are honest men. . . . I sympathize with the poor, but the number of poor who are to be sympathized with is very small. To sympathize with a man whom God has punished for his sins, thus to help him when God would still continue a just punishment, is to do wrong. . . . Let us remember there is not a poor person in the United States who was not made poor by his own shortcomings, or by the shortcomings of someone else. It is all wrong to be poor, anyhow.
>
> *(1915, 18–19, 21)*

For the Founding Fathers, helping the poor wrongs the rich; for Conwell, helping the poor wrongs God.

The popular pontifical transcendentalist, Ralph Waldo Emerson – who excelled at pronouncing trivialities and mystical nonsense with the pomposity of a wise prophet – proudly proclaimed a similarly selfish and dismissive attitude toward those who did not share his prosperous comfort:

> Do not tell me . . . of my obligation to put all poor men in good situations. Are they *my* poor? I tell thee, foolish philanthropist, that I grudge the dollar, the dime, the cent, I give to such men as do not belong to me and to whom I do not belong.
>
> *(1841)*

One of the most popular and well-paid lecturers of his era, Emerson proclaimed slogans of radical individualism and self-sufficiency and selfishness that were central elements of popular American thought. He portrayed himself as a radical "noncomformist" who was hated by the masses: the masses who swarmed to his lectures and cheered his ponderous championing of popular beliefs. Not only did he advocate a "virtuous selfishness," but he also insisted that the deep wisdom of "intuition" – which does not study causes or make critical examinations and is not subject to questioning or deeper examination – is more trustworthy than the views of any experts: intuitions are known with certainty and are "not to be disputed" because they are the direct teachings of the universal "divine spirit." One of those indubitable intuitions – available for the soul that "perceives the self-existence of Truth and Right" – is that "all things go well" that is, we live in a *just world* that is divinely ordered (and it follows that those who prosper and those poor who suffer in this just world are receiving their just deserts – otherwise, things would not be "going well"). And this brave "nonconformist" promoted the popular American myth of the "self-made man": "Welcome evermore to gods and men is the self-helping man. . . . Our love goes out to him and embraces him, because he did not need it" (1841).

In the preeminent land of the free – from the Founders to the present – each person has ample *opportunity* to succeed. No matter your color, your history, your family, your starting point, in America you are responsible for the outcome of your efforts. The market passes final judgment on each person's merits: the best achieve success due to their own individual efforts and abilities, while the worst – due to their own shortcomings – suffer justly deserved ignominious failure. The United States was born with the myth of meritocracy, and the meritocracy myth still flourishes.

4

RUGGED INDIVIDUALISM

America was founded by "Founding Fathers" who were dedicated to radical individualism and "just deserts" (both the morally superior wealthy and the depraved poor justly deserve their different portions). But rather than being ameliorated in later years, in the United States, the radical individualism was strengthened and entrenched and celebrated, from Russell Conwell to Ralph Waldo Emerson to Ronald Reagan to the present. Wendy Brown's *In the Ruins of Neoliberalism* is a brilliant account of the disastrous effects of contemporary neoliberalism and its emphasis on radical individualism: "The assault on society and social justice over the neoliberal decades is most familiar in the project of dismantling and disparaging the social state in the name of free, responsibilized individuals" (2019, 29). Contemporary neoliberalism exacerbated the problem of American radical individualism, but the basic problem is much deeper than the neoliberal forces of the last four decades.

There are several factors that shaped the American culture as a welcoming habitat for neoliberalism, but none is more important or deeply entrenched than the American commitment to *individualism*. The "rugged individual" is not merely a popular image of Western movies but a central theme in American culture: the self-sufficient individual who stands alone and needs no help from anyone, who "makes it on his own," who "takes full responsibility" for his life and actions. The icon is John Wayne, and the theme is typically tied to hyper masculinity.

Because individualism is deeply embedded in American culture, and radical individualism is a central element of neoliberalism, it is not surprising that neoliberalism found a comfortable home in US economic and social thought.

DOI: 10.4324/9781003284680-4

Michael Cavadino and James Dignan make clear the connection between neo-liberalism and individualism:

> The neo-liberal society tends to exclude both those who fail in the economic marketplace and those who fail to abide by the law – in the latter case by means of imprisonment, or even more radically by execution. This is no coincidence. Both types of exclusion are associated with a highly *individualistic* social ethos. This individualistic ethos leads a society to adopt a neo-liberal economy in the first place, but conversely the existence of such an economy in return fosters the social belief that individuals are solely responsible for looking after themselves. In neo-liberal society, economic failure is seen as being the fault of the atomized, free-willed individual, not any responsibility of society – hence the minimal, safety-net welfare state. Crime is likewise seen as entirely the responsibility of the offending individual. The social soil is fertile ground for a harsh 'law and order ideology.'
>
> *(2006, 448)*

But that raises a further question: *why* did American culture become so powerfully individualistic?

The Frontier and Individualism

One possibility is self-selection of those who chose to leave Europe. Alberto Alesina and Edward L. Glaeser suggest that immigration from Europe may have been favored by those more likely to prefer individualist solutions to their difficulties:

> Another possible impact of immigration is the self-selection of those who choose to leave Europe to move to the United States. These immigrants may have had a propensity to find an individual (or individualistic) solution to adversity rather than fomenting a social revolution at home.
>
> *(2004, 9)*

Whatever the influence of immigrant individualism, recent research has shown that American individualism was strengthened by another significant factor: the existence and lure of the American frontier.

Historian Frederick Jackson Turner's "frontier thesis" is one of the most influential themes of American history. It claims that American culture was profoundly and uniquely shaped by the long existence and attraction of its open frontier, which provided special hopes and opportunities for adventurers and homesteaders and pioneers. The frontier thesis was a powerful influence on American historical thought, especially during the late 19th and early 20th centuries. Though Turner's research was subjected to important and legitimate criticism during the late 20th century for his neglect of the important factors of race, gender, and class in frontier life, a recent study (Bazzi, Fiszbein, and Gebresilasse 2017) reveals significant, well-established, and enduring effects of the frontier on American culture. The researchers do not endorse Turner's overall work, noting that his writings "paint an idealized portrait of the frontiersman and leave women and minorities out of the picture" and that Turner describes settlers taking "free land" that was more often the result of conquest (2017, 5). But they have documented some important results from empirical studies inspired by Turner's frontier hypothesis. As they describe the conclusions drawn from their research:

> The frontier fostered the development of distinctive cultural traits, including individualism and opposition to government intervention. The combination of these two traits characterizes "rugged individualism" . . . . Frontier individualism is partly but not entirely explained by selective migration. Frontier conditions favored individualism through higher socioeconomic returns, and they created expectations of high income growth though effort, which fueled opposition to government intervention. . . . In our conceptual framework, the significance of the frontier can be explained by three factors. First, frontier locations attracted individualists able to thrive in harsh conditions. Second, frontier conditions – isolation and low population density – further cultivated self-reliance, and they offered favorable prospects for upward mobility through effort, nurturing hostility to redistribution. Finally, frontier conditions shaped local culture at a critical juncture, thus generating persistent effects.
>
> *(2017, 1)*

As they note, European settlers who risked the journey to the east coast of North America were already moving from settled country to a frontier; and those – their descendants – who sought the risks and rewards farther west were powerfully drawn to the frontier life. Frederick Turner himself stated: "At first, the frontier was the Atlantic coast. It was the frontier of Europe in a very real sense. Moving westward, the frontier became more and more American" (1893).

The most striking result from their research is the strong link between counties that had long periods of "total frontier experience" between 1790 and 1890 and an enduring contemporary attitude of rugged individualism. Counties that remained frontier for longer periods – counties in which (by measures of population density) the frontier endured rather than moving farther west, counties that for various reasons remained frontier rather than becoming settled – continue to this day to have stronger cultures of rugged individualism: including a tendency to support conservative policies such as preference for limited government and low tax levels and opposition to regulation (such as minimum wage levels) and to redistribution of wealth (such as welfare programs). Though the impact is stronger in some areas because of the enduring frontier, the authors conclude that "over the process of westward expansion, the frontier imbued a culture of rugged individualism throughout the US" (2017, 4). The effects of frontier culture remain strong, even under very different conditions. As Bazzi, Fiszbein, and Gebresilasse note:

> Once frontier culture put down roots, it may have persisted through various mechanisms, even if the distinctive features of frontier settlement were long gone. Initial conditions can determine the long-run equilibrium through the dynamics of intergenerational cultural transmission. Moreover, since the frontier shaped culture at the earliest stages, it was bound to influence the formation of local institutions and social identity, which likely affected the subsequent evolution of cultural traits.
>
> *(2017, 25)*

Support for the enduring influence of the frontier experience comes from an unlikely source: a study (Kitayama et al. 2006) conducted thousands of miles from the American frontier, in a culture dramatically different from the culture of frontier America but having a special and striking point of agreement. Until around 1867, Japan's northern island of Hokkaido was a wilderness region inhabited only by small bands of the Ainu, who lived in a hunter-gatherer culture. With the beginning of the Meiji Restoration in 1867, the feudal lords lost power to the emperor and many samurai warriors lost their occupations. The Meiji government feared the expanding power of Russia and its threat to Hokkaido and encouraged the samurai to establish settlements in the Hokkaido "Northern Frontier." Farmers followed the samurai to the Hokkaido frontier, and the population rapidly expanded. Shinobu Kitayama and his colleagues saw an opportunity to study the effects of this "natural experiment" on the development of a "frontier culture" among voluntary settlers of a wilderness region. They hypothesized that Hokkaido would develop a frontier independent culture similar to that of the United States:

> When taken in combination, the three processes – self-selection for settlement, reinforcement of independence during settlement, and institutionalization of tacit beliefs and practices of independence – induce and maintain the ethos of independent agency. This culture of frontier is likely to be resilient and rapidly consolidated because it is created anew, "from scratch," in a place that is relatively separated both from the rest of the world and from its own past.
>
> *(2006, 370)*

The researchers predicted that:

> although Japan traditionally has been governed by a contrasting cultural ethos of interdependence, there will be a strong cultural ethos and spirit of independence in Hokkaido. In this particular respect, Hokkaido Japanese should be more similar to Americans than to mainland Japanese.
>
> *(2006, 371)*

Their prediction was confirmed by their comparative studies of Hokkaido and mainland Japanese:

> Like European Americans in the United States, Hokkaido Japanese embody the spirit of independent agency. These individuals put relatively equal weights on both personal achievement and social harmony. This is in sharp contrast with Japanese in mainland Japan.
>
> *(2006, 374)*

As they conclude, their studies provide:

> evidence that Hokkaido-born Japanese are very similar to Americans. Both of these groups showed a strong bias toward dispositional (as opposed to situational) factors in causal inference [that is, both groups tended to explain behavior in terms of character attributes rather than social environmental influences]. Given these findings and the evidence from the first two studies, we may conclude that there is a strong ethos of independent agency in Hokkaido.
>
> *(2006, 380)*

As in Hokkaido, rugged individualism – with its emphasis on free personal choice and self-sufficiency – was not a temporary trait of American frontier life, but an enduring element of American culture: stronger in some areas than others, but overall, a powerful influence on American thought and politics that shaped a welcoming environment for neoliberalism.

Religion and Individualism

The frontier was not the only factor sustaining and promoting individualism in American culture. Individualism in the American religious culture started early and was linked to the frontier movement. Colonial New England was dominated by Calvinism, while Enlightenment deism was favored by many in the upper classes: God sets things in motion, but is not a personal God, does not answer prayers, and does not take sides in the squabbles and struggles of humans. But while Calvinism and deism are radically different religious perspectives, they share strong opposition to "enthusiasm": the Calvinist Congregationalists because it threatened church authority and established doctrine; the deists because enthusiasm encouraged relying on emotions and rejected the authority of reason. Both groups placed great emphasis on authority, though the source of authority was very different: in the one case, the authority of God as transmitted through the authority of the creed and the church leaders, especially the clergy; in the other, the authority of reason, as trained by elite higher education. Puritan Congregationalists in New England believed that each congregation should be self-governing; nonetheless, the ministers held great authority (both in the individual churches and through their combined influence when they met together), with the ministers of the First Church in Boston (such as John Cotton) having special influence; and they adhered to a creed of belief adopted in London in 1658 (The Savoy Declaration, a revised version of the Westminster Confession of Faith).

In the Protestant tradition, every believer could read the Bible for themselves; but in major Protestant denominations, some – particularly the clergy – had special training and could read it better than others. But one who has a personal, direct, unmediated experience of God – an experience of "the Holy Spirit," which is part of the mysterious Trinity and therefore is a direct experience of God – then that individual *knows* God, beyond any doubts. Even the Bible is not such a direct, personal, intimate, and indubitable revelation of God as is this powerful personal *individual* experience. Having had this direct personal experience of God, no secondhand testimony – whether minister, book, or creed – can improve upon your understanding of God. Those who have direct experience of God may share their experiences with others and preach or witness, but for each person the experience is a highly personal *individual* experience. The only person who fully knows that ecstatic experience is the individual who must rely exclusively on his or her own radically individual self-sufficient knowledge. Those who have had that direct experience may not be able to read Greek or Hebrew – and may struggle with English – but the Holy Spirit is a better source of knowledge and direction than any priest or scholar can offer. American evangelical Christians have a very intimate relation with God. You "place your hand in the nail-scarred hand" of "your dearest friend," and with your divine friend you "walk through the Garden alone, while the dew is still on the roses . . . and He walks with me, and He talks with me, and He tells me that I am his own, and the joy we share, as we tarry there, none other has ever known" (C. Austin Miles, "In the Garden," 1913. With such a friend, who needs a priest?

As Richard Hofstadter notes:

> America is not the only society whose culture has been affected by evangelicalism. But in America, religious culture has been largely shaped by the evangelical spirit, for here the balance of power between

> evangelicalism and formal religion was long ago overwhelmingly tipped in the direction of the former. To see how much this was true one need only compare the historical development of religion in Britain, where the Establishment was prepared to absorb and domesticate a large part of the evangelical movement, with that of America, where the evangelicals rapidly subverted, outstripped, or overwhelmed the older liturgical churches
>
> *(1962, 47)*

The US evangelical movement thrived on a personal emotional relationship with God, and – especially as the distance increased from the established churches of the East coast – the charms of *individual* experiential authority outweighed the strength of church authority. On the frontier there was no external certification, no prescribed orthodoxy, no organization running the church or instructing the individual believers. The authority of any leader depended not on educational or doctrinal or denominational certification, but on charisma. Despised by the leaders of the established New England ministry as heretics and "enthusiasts," they in turn regarded the traditional church leaders as authoritarian obstructions to enlightenment by the Holy Spirit. And as the revivalist movement spread west, it became even more distinct from and independent of the traditional religious authorities. As Richard Hofstadter dramatically describes the process:

> By achieving a religious style congenial to the common man and giving him an alternative to the establishments run by and largely for the comfortable classes, the Awakening quickened the democratic spirit in America; by telling the people that they had a right to hear the kind of preachers that they liked and understood, even under some circumstances a right to preach themselves, the revivalists broke the hold of the establishments and heightened that assertiveness and self-sufficiency which visitor after visitor from abroad was later to find characteristic of the American people. . . . As later revivalism moved from New England and the Middle Colonies and from the Congregational and Presbyterian denominations out into the saddlebag and bear-meat country of the South and the West, it became more primitive, more emotional, and more given to "ecstatic" manifestations.
>
> *(1962, 74)*

There was another source for the popularity of the evangelical movement over the established theological order: the Calvinist doctrines of the establishment Congregational churches were not a good fit with the self-reliant orientation of the frontier. Martin Luther and John Calvin based their doctrines on Biblical texts, particularly passages from St. Paul: gaining salvation (and escaping hell) is not a matter of individual choice but entirely and absolutely a decision made by God – to grant or withhold grace – for God's own inscrutable reasons. Paul makes this position painfully clear:

> Therefore hath he mercy on whom he will have mercy, and whom he will he hardeneth. Thou wilt say then unto me, Why doth he yet find fault? For who hath resisted his will? Nay but, O man, who art thou that repliest against God? Shall the thing formed say to him that formed it, Why hast thou made me thus? Hath not the potter power over the clay, of the same lump to make one vessel unto honour, and another unto dishonour.
>
> *Romans 9:18–21 KJV*

So why does one receive severe eternal punishment, while another is chosen by God to receive grace? It is purely God's decision, and human free willed choice is nonexistent:

> So then it is not of him that willeth, nor of him that runneth, but of God that sheweth mercy.
>
> *Romans 9:16 KJV*

Luther and Calvin emphasize the omniscience and *omnipotence* of almighty God: there is *no* power independent of God's *omni*potence. Humans have no power to choose salvation or damnation; the choice of who is damned and who receives grace is *entirely* God's choice from God's total power. If you receive grace, it is not because of your own choice or act, not by your own *will*, but because God chose to show you mercy. If God chooses not to grant you grace, then you are eternally damned, and there is *nothing* you can do about it. John Calvin did not find this at all troubling; instead – confident he was one of the elect – he looked forward to eternal bliss heightened by the dolorous cries of the damned. Martin Luther *did* find it disturbing, but not so disturbing that it caused him to change his position:

> This is the highest degree of faith – to believe that He is merciful, who saves so few and damns so many; to believe Him just, who according to His own will makes us necessarily damnable . . . . If, therefore, I could by any means comprehend how that same God can be merciful and just who carries the appearance of so much wrath and iniquity, there would be no need of faith. But now, since that cannot be comprehended, there is room for exercising faith …
>
> *1525/1823, section 24*

Resigned faith might work for Luther, but not only did such faith make omnipotent God seem arbitrary and cruel but also made humans utterly helpless. It is one thing to be God's special creation; quite another to be a lowly pot that is controlled, used, and abused for God's inscrutable – and apparently arbitrary – purposes.

For evangelical Americans, salvation is individual, and it is a matter of personal *choice*. Martin Luther, John Calvin, and Jonathan Edwards might insist that (in the words of St. Paul) "it is not of man that chooseth, but of God that calleth;" but Americans were more interested in a do-it-yourself theology. Frontier Americans wanted a better solution, and it came in the form of individual free will. Burning eternally in a lake of fire might seem a rather harsh punishment; but after all, it was your own free choice. The poet AE Housman reported that

> Malt does more than Milton can,
> To justify God's ways to man.

But whatever the benefits of alcoholic beverages, special powers of free will also do a good job of making God's cruel punishments seem just. Jesus is the only path to salvation, but each person makes a special individual uncaused *choice* to take or reject that path. Why do some choose the path of salvation, and others the road to damnation? It is a remarkable first cause godlike choice – we are, after all, made in the image of God – and no prior causes or conditions are relevant. As historian Mark A. Noll notes, evangelists such as Charles Finney (in the early 19th century) went even beyond John Wesley in embracing the believer's special *choice* of salvation: "Wesley maintained that the human will was incapable of choosing God apart from God's preparatory grace, but Finney rejected this requirement" (1992,161).

Rugged individualists made their own way on the frontier through their own choices and efforts – whether the result was success or failure – and insisted their efforts were entirely their own and their own individual responsibility. When the question was their eternal salvation or damnation, they were not willing to leave that choice to anyone else, including God. As Luther had acknowledged, the doctrine of "saved through grace" with no possibility of choice seems fundamentally unfair and unjust. It is not the sort of arbitrary injustice that our special friend, Jesus, would approve; nor is it the teaching of our direct and personal experiences of the Holy Spirit. That accounts for two-thirds of the Trinity, and – for American evangelicals, especially those on the frontier – that was enough, no matter what church authorities might claim.

Although religion in Boston was very different from the religious practices and beliefs of the American frontier, the wealthy New England elite also rejected some traditional Christian doctrines: especially doctrines that called for sharing their wealth with the less fortunate. Along similar lines, although they embraced John Locke's account of the importance and legitimacy of private property, they did *not* accept Locke's view that the very wealthy have an obligation to return their excess wealth to "the commons":

> Since all or most of them [the Founding Fathers] were property owners and of aristocratic bearing either by birth or through education, it was important for them that their status and property interests be protected. And to do this, it was expedient to shed much of the ecclesiastical precepts of the church and the moral imperative of being 'commanded' to share what one has laboured unto oneself. To the extent that worldly possession was a virtue unto itself, the Lockean requirement of forfeiting one's property to the 'commons' above and beyond one's immediate needs was a proposition that ran counter to the founding father's inclination for wealth and private ownership.
>
> *Kalu 2012, 131*

The frontier was a powerful influence on American culture, and its legacy has been celebrated in American songs, stories, movies, and myths. The influence of religion on American culture is also obvious and enduring: the United States has a National Day of Prayer, no disaster happens without politicians rushing out to assure us they are praying for the victims, and both US currency and national anthem proclaim unwavering trust in God. Frontier and religion – and frontier religion – join in support of the radical individualism and personal responsibility at the core of US neoliberalism.

5
FREEDOM

"The word 'freedom' resonates so widely within the common-sense understanding of Americans that it [can] . . . justify almost anything" (Harvey 2005, 39). Critical examination of American "freedom" is not encouraged: the "land of the free" could approve massive slavery, deny voting rights for women, adopt genocidal policies against indigenous peoples, practice mass imprisonment, and sentence impoverished western Massachusetts farmers to debtors' prison. The "freedom" of the proto-neoliberal Founding Fathers and contemporary neoliberals is not freedom from bondage, nor freedom to participate in governance, nor freedom of genuine opportunity; rather, it is freedom to use your property and privileges as you see fit, with no obligations and minimum restrictions. It is freedom to participate in and reap the benefits of the free market if you are wealthy. For others, it is a "freedom" to willingly submit yourself to the judgment of the market and the restraints of your class position.

Thomas Jefferson proclaimed it to be self-evident that all men are endowed by their Creator with the inalienable right of liberty, while also holding slaves and campaigning for the protection and continuation of slavery. That appears to be an egregious inconsistency, but for Jefferson and the other proto-neoliberal founding fathers, there was no conflict (Stovall 2021, 119). It was understood that "all men" who enjoyed the inalienable right of liberty included *only* those who embodied the special characteristics and virtues that enabled them to properly exercise their freedom; and obviously people of color were devoid of those qualities: "Denying freedom to Black slaves was not a contradiction, because freedom was reserved for whites" (Stovall 2021, 119). People of color – along with women and the poor – lack the self-control and wisdom to properly exercise liberty: the right of liberty applies only to those who have the capacity to exercise it properly. Giving "liberty" to those lacking such

DOI: 10.4324/9781003284680-5

virtuous qualities would not enlarge the exercise of liberty but instead encourage profligate and intemperate behavior. Furthermore, slaves were *property*, and the idea of property having a right of liberty was absurd: the basic and preeminent right of property is the right to total control over one's property, which precludes any rights for the property, whether humans, horses, or fields.

From the proto-neoliberal founders to the neoliberal present, the right of "freedom" was understood to apply only to whites. That limit on freedom is tacitly recognized in the racist slogan popular in American films of the mid-twentieth century (Heisel 2015; Lowe 1935): you are "free, white, and twenty-one," and therefore you enjoy freedom, but the rights of freedom do not apply to children or persons of color. The racist reading of "universal freedom" was clear when Senator Jesse Helms – a notorious racist who ran overtly racist campaigns – invoked the same slogan in a 1981 Senate debate: "On the floor we fight hard; we're free, white, and twenty-one, as we say in North Carolina" (quoted in Link 2008, 258). Everyone is endowed by their Creator with the right of liberty; except for those who obviously are not. People of color and the poor (as noted in Chapter 3) are like children, they are "without property and principle," "turbulent and changing," and "they seldom judge or determine right." Their only real "freedom" is the freedom of submission to their betters and to the judgment of the market; anything more is irrational and destructive license, not liberty.

Genuine freedom is the freedom of order, of submission to right authority, the freedom of respect for property and the market, and one's betters. It is not license, it is not freedom from restraint, it is not the freedom of wild exploration and mistakes and adventure. It is not *pirate* freedom (Stovall 2021, 44–50), which knows no rules and respects no property, and is madly egalitarian and democratic. The "freedom" of savages is wild abandon and anarchy: rejection of authority and rules and reason. Such "freedom" must be eradicated in order for genuine freedom – the freedom of order and reason and authority – to thrive. Poor whites lack the self-control and rational ability to properly exercise freedom, but it is a goal to which they can aspire (with the proper guidance); for blacks, it is unimaginable.

The ambiguous use of "liberty" and "freedom" has long been a powerful device for maintaining control of the masses – especially poor whites, who unlike people of color are blessed with at least the potential for "freedom." America is the land of "liberty and justice for all," so long as one does not look too closely at what is signified by "liberty." The appeal to freedom makes a stirring national anthem and a valuable political applause line and an effective political scare tactic ("the abolitionists – or union organizers, or civil rights workers, or socialists – want to *take away your freedom*").

Both the proto-neoliberal Founding Fathers and contemporary neoliberals – Hayek, Friedman, Reagan, Thatcher – needed to offer an attractive benefit, for they knew that many people would suffer from the policies they adopted (and indeed *should* suffer, in their view). What worked for the Founding Fathers also worked for contemporary neoliberals: "An open project around the restoration of economic power to a small elite would probably not gain much popular support. But a programmatic attempt to advance the cause of individual freedoms could appeal to a mass base and so disguise the drive to restore class power" (Harvey 2005, 40).

The masses must learn *submission* to the wisdom of the market and accept the justice of their suffering. *Freedom* and *liberty* and the dignity of *personal responsibility* make the suffering easier to tolerate; and because each person enjoys freedom and complete individual responsibility, people *hope* that by exercising their freedom they can pull themselves up out of poverty and join the elite (and for a significant period, the opening of the "frontier" provided opportunities for the poor to gain some property and escape poverty). The powerful appeal of *freedom* convinces many of the less fortunate that America is the land of opportunity and that they have a great chance of rising to prosperity, although in fact, the United States has become much less economically mobile than most European countries.

The Founding Fathers had another reason for promoting belief in the glories of American *freedom*. They needed to establish grounds for the legitimacy of the new government, and the traditional grounds – the divine right of the rulers – was not available: the new country had just emerged from a rebellion against those divinely ordained powers. The wealthy elite needed a new foundation for its right to govern. The *freedom* of the people in choosing and affirming their government was a glorious new form of legitimate government – indeed, the *only* legitimate basis for government. The new government was justified by *liberty* and the *free* consent of the people.

It wasn't true. Few could vote (suffrage was exclusively for white males with substantial property), and even fewer met the stringent property requirements for holding office. When talking strictly among themselves (behind locked doors in Philadelphia), the founding elite were dedicated to preserving their wealth and preventing the masses of the people from gaining control of the government (for fear that they would redistribute the wealth and property). But that did not deter the Founding Fathers from promising the blessings of liberty and claiming the *authority* of the *free* people whose celebrated affirmation and "equal" participation conferred legitimacy on the government.

Claiming freedom and liberty as the essential justification and shared benefit of the new nation had another great advantage for the proto-neoliberal Founding Fathers. If the people demanded any real control of the government, then emphasis on the *freedom* of the American people could be used to deflect their attention from the question of who actually held the power of governing (and how meager was the share of government controlled by the people). Elbridge Gerry was one of only two delegates to the Constitutional Convention who refused to sign the proposed constitution, believing it concentrated too much power in the hands of the elite and contained inadequate safeguards against the government evolving into an aristocracy. Gerry demanded that a bill of rights be added to the Constitution, but he considered the Bill of Rights contained in the first ten amendments to be wholly inadequate for providing the needed protections. As Michael J. Klarman notes:

> Gerry considered them [the Bill of Rights] plainly irrelevant to whether the "Constitution will preserve its theoretical balance" or else tilt toward aristocracy or monarchy, and he thought the amendments would serve no purpose other than "to reconcile those who had no adequate idea of the essential defects of the Constitution."
>
> *Klarman 2016, 594*

Most of the founders had no objection to the new country "tilting toward aristocracy," and they were confident that nothing in the Bill of Rights would prevent such an outcome. The rights enshrined in the Bill of Rights – rights of free speech and free assembly and freedom of religion and free press – are valuable, but they do little to limit the entrenched power and control of a governing elite. But the Bill of Rights celebrated individual *freedoms*, and the promise of freedom was and is an effective palliative against concerns about the concentrated power of a small elite governing on behalf of their own interests.

Neoliberal "Freedom"

When a system is celebrated as supporting *freedom* and liberty for all, then the entire system is bathed in that magical glow, and any criticisms or doubts are cast as attacks on freedom. The charms of "freedom" are much needed when trying to sell the US constitution (which protected elitism, not to mention slavery) and a "free market" system that concentrates more power and more wealth in fewer and more privileged hands. Both the proto-neoliberal founders and contemporary neoliberals place great emphasis on "freedom." But freedom is an empty promise without real opportunity and support. We are not "self-made men," and we need the right conditions and tools and workshops and opportunities and training and protection to effectively exercise freedom.

"Freedom" is the basis for the false claim of equal opportunity: "equal opportunity" in a fair contest in which winners and losers receive their just deserts. It sounds democratic and fair and egalitarian: We don't care about your background or your social status, it's what you do now that counts. Like a race, where we all start "even," but some have special racing shoes, great coaches, superb nutrition, and state-of-the-art training facilities. In one sense, the race is fair and the start is even; but on deeper inquiry, the start was substantially staggered. We all "start fair" in the race, but the advantages and disadvantages are built into the contest.

Orestes Brownson, a 19th-century American reformer and writer, made clear the problem of unequal starts and the emptiness of the claim that the race is fair because all the participants are "free":

> all the members of the community should have, so far as society is concerned, equal chances. But equal chances imply equal starting points. Nobody . . . could pretend that where the points of departure were unequal the chances could be equal. Do the young man inheriting ten thousand pounds, and the one whose inheritance is merely the gutter, start even? Have they equal chances? It may be said both are free to rise as high as they can,– one starting with ten thousand pounds in advance, and the other starting with the gutter. But it might as well be said the chances of the eldest son of the Duke of Newcastle, and those of the eldest son of one of the Duke's tenants, are equal, since both unquestionably are free to rise as high as they can,– one starting with a dukedom in advance, and the other with nothing.
>
> *Brownson 1840, 394*

George Sher proposes a solution to the problem of "fair starts":

> Even if M is initially stronger or more intelligent than N, this difference will only entail that M does not deserve what he has achieved relative to N if the difference between them has made it impossible for N to achieve as much as M. However, differences in strength, intelligence, and other native gifts are rarely so pronounced as to have this effect. The far more common effect of such differences is merely to make it more *difficult* for the less talented person to reach a given level of attainment. He must work harder, husband his resources more carefully, plan more shrewdly, and so on.
>
> *(1987, 31–32)*

Sher's proposed solution to the problem of fair starts builds in a false assumption of basic fairness: while people may vary in the beneficial attributes and abilities they possess, the overall combination of abilities balances out: the "less talented" person may overcome that disadvantage through superior fortitude and planning.[1] But as exensive research makes clear (Wolff and De-Shalit 2007), disadvantages – especially the strong "corrosive disadvantages" – are not distributed randomly but tend to *cluster* together and have a powerful detrimental impact on lives. The person of less talent is likely to have more trouble working harder and planning shrewdly. To take a simple example, the initially less talented athlete is more likely to become discouraged and find it more difficult to exert effort, and because the inferior athlete plays less, she is unlikely to develop "court savvy" and plan shrewdly, and is less likely to be selected for elite teams with better coaches who teach her how to improve her game and play with greater confidence. Like the delightful story of the resilient tortoise and the lethargic hare, Sher's account of the player whose dedicated efforts compensate for deficient talents is a nice fit with our deep nonconscious belief in a just world; but when examined closely, it remains a charming children's story but an implausible support for fair starts and moral responsibility.

Freedom is wonderful, and we should work to enhance it, but the very charm and importance of freedom make it an attractive device for justifying exploitation and denying genuine opportunity. The Founding Fathers celebrated liberty, but property was always more important than liberty: escaped slaves were property that must be returned to its rightful owners, and the few founders who favored emancipation always included the right of slave owners to be compensated for their property. From the proto-neoliberalism of the Founding Fathers to contemporary Reagan neoliberalism, the talk is of liberty, but the practice promotes slavery and commitment to property and privilege.

Positive and Negative Freedom

"Freedom" has many proposed meanings, and often they are in conflict. There is "freedom" for the governing privileged and "freedom as submission" for others; freedom as having basic personal rights distinguished from freedom as self-governance; and there is a distinction between positive and negative senses of freedom. Neoliberals (and proto-neoliberals) emphasize *negative* freedom: the freedom *from interference*. This includes above all the freedom from interference with private property: freedom from regulation, freedom from the threat of redistribution, freedom to use one's property as one wishes with no impediments or obligations. But it also includes negative freedoms against interference in free speech, free exercise of religion, freedom of the press, and free assembly. This is the *negative* freedom of Isaiah Berlin (1969) that he calls negative liberty. Negative freedom is important: there are good reasons to minimize interference in our freedom of speech and religion and assembly; and both personal security and a functioning market require limits on interference with private property. But there are also important values that require *positive* freedom: a freedom of real choices, effective control, and genuine opportunity requires positive protection from hunger, homelessness, despair, poverty, disease; and it requires the conditions that are essential for genuine opportunity, including education and health care. As Egyptian President Gamal Abdal Nasser noted, it is essential that we see "Freedom as more than liberty of thought and speech and writing. It is the liberty of a full stomach, a good home, health, education, work, security in old age" (quoted in Moyn 2018, 101). Positive *freedom* is not a negative collection of "thou shalt not" rules: rules against taking private property, against interference in freedom of speech and assembly and religion. And positive freedom is not a mysterious "freedom" that somehow makes one morally responsible for all failures, lack of opportunity notwithstanding.

Not only are negative freedom and positive freedom distinct senses of freedom, but they can – as Berlin emphasized – come into conflict. The negative freedom of unlimited and unregulated use of the power of private property can result in deceptive and monopolistic practices that damage the positive freedom of opportunity for those with fewer resources: when a powerful company has monopolistic control over a segment of the "free" market, then there is little opportunity to launch a new venture in that domain. Negative freedom can and does result in environmental harms that compromise the health and well-being and freedom of others. The "freedom" to rent or sell or provide service to or hire whomever one chooses – and *deny* service or housing or jobs – is a freedom to abuse, a freedom to lock some into second-class status, a freedom to deny fair and equal opportunity. That "freedom" to do as one wishes with one's own business or property is a power to demean and mistreat. "We reserve the right to refuse service to anyone" means that we reserve the right to treat some people unjustly, we reserve the power to block some from respect and dignity and fair opportunity and a decent life. Property rights are valuable, but absolute "property rights" promote injustice. The "right" to sell or rent your property to anyone you wish is the "right" to sustain racism and perpetuate segregation.

There can be no *positive* freedom of opportunity without widely available and excellent educational and health care and nutritional and housing resources, but funding such resources requires taxes that "interfere" with the absolute negative freedom of private property possession. There are serious and difficult questions concerning whether the negative right of free speech should be limited to prevent demeaning hate speech that undermines the positive freedom of opportunity and safety of those who are victimized: questions that cause hard struggles for society, including universities. And in a political system that allows the wealthy to use their property for unlimited spending on massive campaign donations, high-priced lobbyists, and almost monopolistic domination of the marketplace of ideas, the positive freedom of most people to have a genuine voice in their government is severely compromised if not destroyed. Negative freedom is important; but for those who value genuine opportunity and enhancing the capacity of exercising effective control, positive freedom also has a strong claim on our allegiance.

Note

1 In a later work Sher (2006) abandons efforts to show that holding people morally responsible is fair, and instead argues *against* what he calls the fairness principle, claiming that it is quite legitimate to hold people responsible even though it violates the fairness standard. Sher's arguments are discussed in Waller 2011, 167–170.

6

MORAL RESPONSIBILITY

Proto-neoliberals and contemporary neoliberals in the United States share a common problem: how can a country in which it is "self-evident" that "all men are created equal" justify enormous differences in wealth? Differences between wealthy Boston patricians and impoverished Western Massachusetts farmers, between magnificent estates and crowded tenements, between luxurious mansions and widespread homelessness? In the face of severe economic hardship and grossly inequitable distribution of wealth, how can the privileged make neoliberalism appear beneficial and just?

As noted earlier, Captain Nathaniel Chipman offered the proto-neoliberal solution: "Wealth, or at least, a competency, is the reward, provided by the laws of nature, for prudent industry; want, the punishment of idleness and profligacy" (Chipman 1793). Contemporary neoliberals use different terms, but the basic idea is the same. Todd Zywicki champions the "personal responsibility" political ideology: "The personal responsibility ideology sees consumer bankruptcy as primarily a moral issue, rather than an economic issue" (2003, 2026). Under neoliberal "personal responsibility," both wealth and poverty are *justly deserved*. As Jessica Whyte notes: "The Chicago economists were deeply aware of the non-economic prerequisites for their preferred market order. If romanticism and demagoguery were the greatest barriers to 'good economics', a working market order required market subjects responsible for their own fates" (2019a, 173). Riches and poverty are the result of the virtues and vices of people who are "personally responsible" for those outcomes.

Moral responsibility and just deserts furnish neoliberals with a convenient explanation for why the wealthy prosper and take such a disproportionate share of the wealth while the poor are destitute: the wealthy prosper

DOI: 10.4324/9781003284680-6

because they are morally superior, and they have earned their just rewards by their exemplary work and character; while the poor are receiving their just deserts for their laziness, bad habits, poor planning, and general bad character and actions. The free competitive market is the sole judge of character and worth. Its positive judgment is signified by wealth and its objectively true negative judgment is indicated by poverty. And because (as noted in Chapter 2) our nonconscious belief in a just world strongly inclines us to believe that the way the world distributes benefits and burdens is basically just, the neoliberal claim – wealth is a clear mark of virtue – starts with a big advantage.

Moral responsibility is the philosopher's stone that transmutes apparent injustice and unfairness into the bright gold of virtue, and – joining forces with belief in a just world – explains away the supposed unjust treatment of the poor: the poor are morally corrupt and are suffering their just deserts for their morally vile behavior. It is no accident that the neoliberal United States has the strongest commitment to individual moral responsibility together with brutally overcrowded prisons and a shredded safety net. As noted earlier, Cavadino and Dignan draw the clear connection:

> In neo-liberal society, economic failure is seen as being the fault of the atomized, free-willed individual, not any responsibility of society – hence the minimal, safety-net welfare state. Crime is likewise seen as entirely the responsibility of the offending individual. The social soil is fertile ground for a harsh 'law and order ideology.'
>
> *(2006, 448)*

Radical individualism is a key element of the American devotion to individual moral responsibility. The extreme John Wayne "rugged individualism" celebrated in US myths and western movies encourages belief in self-making and individual responsibility for who you are and what you achieve, and it strongly *dis*courages any deeper inquiry into the forces that shaped you and continue to influence you. I "made it myself" (with no help from anyone) was a campaign slogan in the Republican attack on Barack Obama during his reelection campaign. Obama touched a sensitive nerve when he stated a plain truth that self-made individuals hate to acknowledge:

> If you were successful, somebody along the line gave you some help. There was a great teacher somewhere in your life. Somebody helped to create this unbelievable American system that we have that allowed you to thrive. Somebody invested in roads and bridges. If you've got a business – you didn't build that. Somebody else made that happen.
>
> *White House, Office of the Press Secretary 2012*

Self-made men deserve all the credit and owe nothing to society or to anyone. The claim is pathetic, but also profoundly harmful. Moral responsibility claims rest on the same belief: the buck stops *here*.

The American culture has a long history of radical individualism and moral responsibility: a much stronger commitment than is found in Europe. In comparison to Europe and Canada, the United States also exhibits great enthusiasm for harsh punishment: it imprisons at a rate several times that of most European countries, continues to carry out executions although most European countries eliminated the death penalty several decades ago, and its prisons are notoriously cruel (employing psychologically harmful punishments such as long-term solitary confinement). Belief in imposing severe *just deserts* on offenders is unusually strong in the United States. No ambitious US politician can risk being labeled "soft on crime," and political opponents often compete to see who can voice the harshest "law and order" rhetoric. When combined with subtle (or overt) racism, a law-and-order campaign is a popular and often effective political ploy.

Neoliberal Moral Responsibility

Moral responsibility bestows the blessing of justly deserved reward onto wealth and privilege and preserves the threatened belief in a just world. Small wonder, then, that belief in moral responsibility appears intuitively obvious and provides a deep foundation for the neoliberal system. Though neoliberal commitment to moral responsibility is strong, the long-sought *justification* for moral responsibility is weak. Even a brief survey of the full range of desperate efforts to support moral responsibility would require volumes: they are legion. Their sheer number raises questions about their plausibility: had someone fashioned a solid argument in support of moral responsibility, there would not be such a remarkable range of failed attempts.

The most popular and basic argument for moral responsibility is the *causa sui* argument: humans have the special capacity to make *choices* that literally make us *causes of ourselves*. When making such self-creating choices we are – like God – *first* causes, and there are *no* prior causes in our characters, environments, histories, or values. The godlike self-making creative choices are inexplicable other than being self-caused. Because we *make ourselves* by our own special uncaused choices, we are totally responsible for the characters we make and the acts we perform.

Unfortunately for *causa sui* aspirations, the notion of *causa sui* powers is incoherent. Nietzsche made the problems brutally clear:

> The *causa sui* is the best self-contradiction that has been conceived so far, it is a sort of rape and perversion of logic; but the extravagant pride of man has managed to entangle itself profoundly and frightfully with just

> this nonsense. . . . The desire to bear the entire and ultimate responsibility for one's actions . . . involves nothing less than to be precisely this *causa sui* and . . . to pull oneself up into existence by the hair, out of the swamps of nothingness.
>
> *Nietzsche 1966, section 21*

A *causa sui* choice is independent of my desires, values, character, needs, preferences, environment. It is difficult to imagine how that could be *my* choice at all. *Causa sui* choice may be a perversion of logic, and self-contradictory; but it has powerful appeal, especially when the need to justify moral responsibility and just deserts is strong and belief in a just world is at stake.

Both proto and contemporary neoliberals place great store in personal responsibility, and in the *just deserts* doled out by the free market. But neither devote much attention to the grounds for moral responsibility and just deserts. What matters is the behavior: is it industrious or lethargic, wise or foolish, effective or incompetent? *Why* one is industrious and sagacious while another is indolent and foolish: that is not explored. That refusal to inquire at greater depth – into the forces and factors that shaped different characters and abilities —is enshrined as principle. Ronald Reagan, the political "founding father" of contemporary neoliberalism in the United States, made that clear: "Our forebears [who believed in moral responsibility] were never concerned about why a person misbehaves. We are straying from the principle of holding the individual responsible for his actions" (quoted in Beckett 1997, 66). If one is self-made, or *causa sui*, then looking for deeper causes is futile. When moral responsibility is based on miraculous *causa sui* or first cause powers, then obviously any deeper inquiry comes to a grinding halt: there *are* no deeper or earlier causal factors to examine if one is a *first* cause or pure *self*-cause.

Self-making is central to neoliberalism, and devotion to the self-made "rugged individual" is very powerful in the neoliberal US. Neoliberals emphasize the autonomous rational person who is fully responsible for his or her "investment" decisions. When the market results of those autonomous rational self-determined investments are positive, the rational individual has earned the benefits; when the autonomous choice is bad, the autonomous individual justly deserves to suffer the results, whether poverty or prison. The buck *stops* with the choices of the autonomous individual. As Trent Hamann notes, under neoliberalism: "Exploitation, domination, and every other form of social inequality is rendered invisible *as social* phenomena to the extent that each individual's social condition is judged as nothing other than the effect of his or her own choices and investments" (2009, 43). The better people just *are* better and choose better and act better, and therefore are justly deserving of reward. The market outcome confirms that judgment and the market is the final arbiter. In our neoliberal meritocracy, the best people rise to the top and reap their just rewards.

Many contemporary philosophers have promoted accounts of moral responsibility that support the neoliberal model. That is not to suggest that they embrace the neoliberal system (including deep cuts in social welfare support and harsh criminal justice policies and blind faith in the unregulated free market): most do not, and are more likely repulsed by those policies. But their efforts to defend moral responsibility support the principles and program of neoliberalism.

While few contemporary philosophers endorse overtly miraculous *causa sui* free will powers, the charms of *causa sui* still have strong appeal. Daniel Dennett is no friend of miracles, but he finds the basic *self-making* model of moral responsibility attractive:

> I take responsibility for any thing I make and then inflict upon the general public; if my soup causes food poisoning, or my automobile causes air pollution, or my robot runs amok and kills someone, I, the manufacturer, am to blame. . . . I am held responsible for releasing the product to the public with whatever flaws it has. Common wisdom has it that much the same rationale grounds personal responsibility; I have created and unleashed an agent who is myself; if its acts produce harm, the manufacturer is held responsible. I think this common wisdom is indeed wisdom . . .
>
> *(1984, 85)*

Robert Kane 2007, 1998; Kane (1985) struggles to fashion a version of self-making that rejects all appeals to miraculous powers, relying instead on quantum indeterminacy amplified by chaos that is generated by deliberative struggle. Adina Roskies also favors self-making (she calls it self-authorship) as grounds for moral responsibility. Her account emphasizes a long process of self-making that is heavily dependent on careful deliberation:

> Through deliberately thinking and acting in strategic ways we can exert control, modulate and intervene in our future states, both physical and mental. It is this that allows us to shape ourselves in ways that make it the case that we are in some very real sense responsible for who we are.
>
> *(2012, 331)*

This need not be the self-making from the ground (or the swamp) up:

> It is not necessary to create oneself out of whole cloth. Continual shaping of the given over time establishes sufficient control of the agent to suffice as a grounding kind of self-causation.
>
> *(2012, 338)*

The idea of self-making has undeniable appeal, and there is no doubt that we do – for better or worse – engage in some degree of self-making. When

I binge-watch television while eating mass quantities of junk food, I make myself more lethargic, passive, and dull. When I persevere in a rigorous program of exercise or study, I shape myself to be more alert, energetic, and even imaginative. In this and many other ways, we can and do engage in "continual shaping" and some degree of self-making. Roskies insists that when we reach "the decision of the agent" then "that is the appropriate place to stop" and we should make no further or deeper inquiry into the decision-making process: "the buck stops here" (2012, 333). She claims that if we push the inquiry further, we wind up with neuropsychological causes, and that is not the appropriate level of inquiry. Roskies is correct that if we are to preserve belief in moral responsibility, we must call a halt to deeper inquiries that swiftly undermine the plausibility of that belief. But she is wrong that inquiring further takes us to the realm of neuropsychological processes. Inquiries that come nowhere near the neuropsychological level are clearly relevant, and they soon demolish the hope that self-making can support claims of moral responsibility.

Roskies insists that halting inquiry at the point of the agent's choice is not an arbitrary stopping point, but instead a stopping point appropriately based on the powers of deliberative reason:

> Certainly, our reasons may be elements of us that are in some sense given. But they are not unchangeable. The agent, in appreciating the content of a reason, can intervene in the way in which that reason operates in his deliberation, in loops of agential control. If he or she did not, and by not doing so the agent accepted and endorsed that reason and its role in his deliberation, then . . . that is the appropriate place to stop. Agents control themselves via conscious access to mental content. We therefore have a convenient way of locating the source of the control: at the agentive, aware level.
>
> *(2012, 334–335)*

But a brief inquiry into the nature of the agent's deliberation at the "agentive, aware level" reveals the shallowness of that stopping point. In the first place, the "agentive aware level" is blind to many vitally important psychological factors. Psychological research (Davies 2019; Dehaene 2014; Kahneman 2011; Wilson 2002) has made that abundantly clear, but the prophet Jeremiah did not require those fascinating studies to recognize that our agentive deliberative decisions are often blind to decisive causal factors and that we often deceive ourselves concerning our own motives and reasons: "The heart is deceitful above all things, and desperately wicked: who can know it?" (Jeremiah 17:9 KJV) What Jeremiah knew millennia ago contemporary psychologists have confirmed and elaborated in important ways. Rather than agentive unbiased fully conscious deliberation determining our choices, much of our deliberation is rationalization to justify what we wish to do for nonconscious emotional motives. Jonathan Haidt describes the actual largely nonconscious process:

> Automatic processes run the human mind, just as they have been running animal minds for 500 million years, so they're very good at what they do, like software that has been improved through thousands of product cycles. When human beings evolved the capacity for language and reasoning at some point in the last million years, the brain did not rewire itself to hand over the reins to a new and inexperienced charioteer. Rather, the rider (language-based reasoning) evolved because it did something useful for the elephant.
>
> The rider . . . acts as the spokesman for the elephant, even though it doesn't necessarily know what the elephant is really thinking. The rider is skilled at fabricating post hoc explanations for whatever the elephant has just done, and it is good at finding reasons to justify what the elephant wants to do next. Once human beings developed language and began to use it to gossip about each other, it became extremely valuable for elephants to carry on their backs a full-time public relations firm.
>
> *(2012, 45–46)*

Haidt and Jeremiah make clear the implausibility of an "agentive, aware level" at which "agents control themselves via conscious access to mental content." There are many factors that influence and often distort the reasoned deliberation we imagine to be unbiased and transparent and totally under our special conscious control. First, the capacity for engaging and sustaining our "System 2" (Kahneman 2011) powers of careful deliberation varies widely. It is a popular misconception that almost everyone can always think longer and harder and deeper, and it is a misconception that is especially popular among philosophers. The eminent philosopher Charles Taylor celebrated our ubiquitous powers of radical self-evaluation and "self-resolution": "Because this self-resolution [deep self-evaluation] is something we do when we do it, we can be called responsible for ourselves; and because it is within limits always up to us to do it, even when we don't – indeed, the nature of our deepest evaluations constantly raises the question of whether we have them right – we can be called responsible in another sense for ourselves whether we undertake this radical evaluation or not" (1976, 299). When Jonathan Haidt gave research subjects cases in which they already favored a specific ethical conclusion, but in which all the grounds in support of their favored view were conclusively blocked, the subjects would reluctantly acknowledge the failure of their given reasons for their favored view but still insist that their view was correct and that there *must* be good reasons in support of it. As Haidt describes the uncomfortable "reasoning" of the subjects:

> These subjects were reasoning. They were working quite hard at reasoning. But it was not reasoning in search of truth; it was reasoning in support of their emotional reactions.
>
> *(2012, 25)*

If we do engage in "self-resolution," it is more likely to be a rationalization of our values than a transparent objective deliberative evaluation. But in addition, Taylor's view that "it is within limits always up to us to do it [deep self-evaluation], even when we don't" is philosophical fantasy. There are large differences in the capacity for System 2 deliberation: differences in what researchers' label "need for cognition" (Cohen, Stotland, and Wolfe 1955). "Chronic cognizers" engage more frequently in deliberative efforts and sustain them longer, while "cognitive misers" find System 2 deliberation more aversive and abandon it quickly (Cacioppo and Petty 1982). Those differences in degrees of need for cognition are important: Chronic cognizers are more open to new experiences (Olson, Camp, and Fuller 1984), they deliberate longer and harder (Osberg 1987) and they are more proficient at solving complex problems (Nair and Ramnarayan 2000). That difference stems from early conditioning histories:

> Children who learn, through observation and experience, that they can cope with their problems through reason and verbal influence rather than through physical force or flight should tend to develop higher levels of need for cognition because of the demonstrated import of good problem-solving skills in charting a course through the hazards of life.
>
> *Cacioppo et al. 1996, 246*

Not only are there large differences in need for cognition but also important variations in *confidence* in one's ability to reason effectively. Albert Bandura describes differences in *cognitive self-efficacy* (Bandura 1997): the degree of confidence in one's ability to successfully solve problems and discover better paths by careful deliberation. After repeated failures in vigorous cognitive efforts (such as early childhood attempts at difficult cognitive challenges that were beyond the child's abilities) cognitive self-efficacy is severely weakened. The frustrating student who "won't even try" to solve a challenging logic problem may be incapable of making such an effort. The "willful refusal" to exert effort is obvious; the harsh history that shaped such cognitive helplessness is invisible. Like Charles Taylor, Roskies is a chronic cognizer surrounded by chronic cognizers, and – with good grounds – she has a strong sense of her own cognitive self-efficacy. When she generalizes from her own case, it is not surprising that the result is misjudgment of the wide range in both need for cognition and cognitive self-efficacy.

Roskies' confident assertion that "Agents control themselves via conscious access to mental content" is a common but false view of our cognitive operations. Michael Gazzaniga's view is jarring to our "common sense" beliefs but much more accurate: "Our conscious awareness is the mere tip of the iceberg of nonconscious processing" (2011, 68). Researchers have confirmed the powerful force of nonconscious cognitive operations, but such operations are also demonstrated by common experience. We struggle to remember a name and our conscious thought dismisses the query, only to have the nonconscious cognitive gears spit out the name when we "are no longer thinking about it." We engage in an intense but unresolved dispute and "forget all about it," but the next day our continuing nonconscious processing supplies our conscious thought with a knock-down argument. The brilliant solution to a mathematical challenge comes to Henri Poincaré out of the blue, when he had "set the problem aside" from his conscious deliberation (and trusted his nonconscious reasoning to work out the extraordinarily difficult solution). Psychological research reveals the profound but almost entirely nonconscious influence of belief in a just world. Stereotyping (Kunda and Spencer 2003; Nosek et al. 2007) is especially destructive because it typically operates without our conscious awareness (and often despite our conscious denial). Unconscious confirmation bias can confound even careful researchers. Seemingly trivial *situational* factors – such as the encouragement of an authority figure, who influences two-thirds of subjects to inflict what they thought might be a fatal series of high voltage shocks (Milgram 1963) – exert profound influence on our thought and behavior, causing us to perform acts that we *consciously* insist we would not do under any circumstances.

Adina Roskies is no doubt aware of the many factors that undercut claims of the transparency of our deliberative decisions and choices; so why would she rest her claim for moral responsibility on the reliability of a special "agentive, aware level"? One problem is that Roskies is overly enamored of what she calls "the folk metaphysics of agency" (2012, 335): on that "folk metaphysics" view "agents control themselves via conscious access to mental content." The belief in the transparency and power of our conscious reasoning is sufficiently common to warrant the title of "the folk metaphysics of agency," but common as that view may be, it is no more reliable than "the folk metaphysics of creationism," which is equally devoid of scientific support.

There is another closely related problem. Roskies is charmed by "the folk metaphysics of agency" because she succumbs to a rationalist temptation that is ubiquitous among the "chronic cognizers" who make up the philosophical tribe. From Aristotle to Kant to the present, the power of reason has been represented as a transparent uniquely human godlike power that can transcend all impediments. Bad reasoning is due to the reasoner's willful neglect – or, from the neoliberal perspective, due to risky and intemperate investment decisions – not a limit in the power of reason itself. Roskies' celebration of the special powers of reason is evident: "The agent, in appreciating the content of a reason, can intervene in the way in which that reason operates in his deliberation, in loops of agential control." Whatever the starting point or history or influences (conscious or nonconscious) the rational agent "can intervene" through a deliberative process – in wondrous "loops of agential control" – to neutralize any obstacles to the remarkable power of conscious reason. It is an inspiring story, and a worthy addition to Aristotle's view that "reason is divine" and empowers humans to "make ourselves immortal," but the Aristotelian view of human reason and contemporary versions of that view have the same plausibility as the Aristotelian account of biology.

Christine Korsgaard is a brilliant and insightful advocate of Kantian rationalism, but – consistently with Kant – her account of human transparent reason makes the power of reason more like the traditional *causa sui* power than anything psychologists would recognize as the limited and often deceived human cognitive powers. According to Korsgaard, "When you deliberate, when you determine your own causality, it is as if there is something over and above all your incentives, something which is *you*, and which chooses which incentive to act on" (2009, 72). "Determining your own causality" through a power of reason that "is something over and above all your incentives" sounds like the transcendent *first cause* powers that have traditionally propped up belief in moral responsibility. Such powers have wonderful appeal for humans who wish to celebrate our unique godlike nature, and they seem obvious to neoliberals who assume we all employ special powers of autonomous reason, but they run aground on the shoals of empirical investigation.

Harry Frankfurt developed an account of moral responsibility that decisively rejects all special miraculous choices that would violate a determinist world view: "The principle of alternate possibilities is false. A person may well be morally responsible for what he has done even though he could not have done otherwise" (1969, 832). Frankfurt insists that a person may be morally responsible for an act even if it was impossible for that person to have acted differently. The important requirement is not open possibilities, but reflective higher-order *affirmation* of one's act or character:

> To the extent that a person identifies himself with the springs of his actions, he takes responsibility for those actions and acquires moral responsibility for them; moreover, the question of how the actions and his identifications with their springs is caused is irrelevant to the questions of whether he performs the actions freely or is morally responsible for performing them.
>
> *(1975, 122)*

It is not surprising that Frankfurt's account has become philosophically popular. First, it purports to justify moral responsibility, something most philosophers fervently desire; second, it avoids the problem of radically alternate possibilities (which are difficult to reconcile with our understanding of scientific causation); third, it assigns a prominent role to higher-order reflective reason, which is very dear to philosophers; and finally, it emphasizes the decisive *willing* of reflective approval, and the power of *will* (along with reason) has long had philosophical charms.

The delights of Frankfurt's moral responsibility account notwithstanding, scrutiny reveals fatal flaws. Frankfurt's insistence that "how the actions and her identifications with their springs is caused is irrelevant" is an essential element in efforts to preserve belief in moral responsibility. Deeper inquiry soon reveals causal factors of great importance in shaping character and behavior: causes such as a weak sense of self-efficacy, frail powers of fortitude, low need for cognition, nonconscious beliefs and stereotypes, and powerful but unrecognized situational influences that were clearly not under the control of the individual. When we consider the enormous influence of "luck" on the ways our characters develop and our behavior is influenced (Levy 2011; Nagel 1979), then we destroy the easy confidence that either "self-making" or self-affirmation can justify claims of moral responsibility. If we want to preserve moral responsibility, we must block inquiry; and if we value deeper inquiry, we must move beyond the myopia promoted by belief in moral responsibility.

The "rugged individual" who is self-made and self-reliant is as basic to neoliberalism as it is to classic Western movies. It was popular among proto-neoliberals who wished to claim full responsibility for their wealth and privileges and power, it was reinforced by the frontier experience, and it flourishes among contemporary neoliberals and in the popular imagination – and contemporary philosophers are not immune to its charms. Deeper inquiry makes the fatal problems obvious. That is why neoliberals insist we should not look deeper, and philosophers who defend moral responsibility insist that deeper examination is irrelevant.

Limiting Inquiry and Saving Moral Responsibility

A common theme among advocates of moral responsibility is an insistence on calling a halt to deeper investigation: "the buck stops here" and further inquiry is irrelevant and can only lead to confusion. John Martin Fischer's work is fascinating and insightful, but his defense of moral responsibility ultimately depends on one basic principle: don't look deeper. Fischer characterizes the insistence that we inquire deeper into the *causes* of character and behavior as "metaphysical megalomania" (2007, 67): a desire to push deeper – much too deep, according to Fischer – into understanding *why* people choose and act as they do.

Fischer insists that a modest level of control suffices for moral responsibility:

> Just as an astronaut may still control the lift-off of the rocket, even though she did not build the platform that makes the launch possible (or ever have any control over the platform), we can be accountable for playing the cards that are dealt us, even if we did not manufacture the cards, write the rules of the game, and so forth. We can exercise precisely that sort of control of our behavior that moral responsibility requires, without having an inflated or exalted power of self-creation. It is a kind of wisdom . . . to recognize that, when you play the cards that are dealt you (in a certain distinctive way), you can exercise a robust sort of control, even in the absence of the power to make the cards, to own the factory that makes the cards, to make up the rules of the game, and so forth.
>
> *Fischer 2012, 185*

But focusing on the way *you* play the cards you've been dealt and how *you* pilot your space launch blocks a critically important level of inquiry: *why* do you have or lack the skill to "play your cards successfully" and make the best of your situation? The level of your ability to "play your cards successfully" is – unless we are capable of *causa sui* miracles – the result of your history: a history (perhaps including your genetic history) that shaped your self-efficacy, your need for cognition, your capacity for self-control and fortitude, your confidence, your optimism (or pessimism). We all admire the player who plays her cards with confidence, skill, fortitude, and "savvy," but it does not follow that the admirable player is *morally responsible* for the abilities that make her successful, and even brief reflection reveals the many ways she was shaped by forces she neither chose nor controlled. Your skill at "playing the cards that were dealt you" is among the cards you were dealt.

Efforts to block deeper examination of the causes of behavior are common practice in desperate defenses of moral responsibility, and Fischer develops a particularly elegant version. He claims that we should follow the "middle way" (2012, 20) in our consideration of moral responsibility. That is, we should not return to the "eye for an eye" punitive extreme in which there is no room for excuses (excuses such as accident or madness), but neither should we go too far in the other direction and examine the deeper causes for why one chooses and acts in a vicious or virtuous manner. The correct "middle way" is to focus on the current behavior and character and any systemically approved excuses recognized by our moral responsibility system (excuses such as immaturity, dementia, madness, coercion), and make sure that the act really came from the individual's own competent choice, and that's where the inquiry should *stop*: no extreme inquiries into environmental or family or genetic or any other causal factors that shaped the individual's character and desires and abilities. This is simply to say – when the "middle way" elegance is cleared away – that we should cling to our basic system of moral responsibility, and not consider any deep challenges to that system. Fischer's program has advantages. To borrow a line from Bertrand Russell, it has all the advantages of theft over honest labor.

Neoliberalism, Just Deserts, and Ending Inquiry

There is a difference between proto-neoliberals and contemporary neoliberals on the question of just deserts, but the difference is more in perspective than substance. Proto-neoliberals were quite willing to equate wealth with virtue and use that assumed virtue to claim that their wealth was *justly deserved* and that their superior qualities entitled them to positions of privilege and authority: as the wealthy were clearly the wise and virtuous, it was obvious that they should hold political power. But neoliberal theorists such as Hayek and Friedman do not embrace such a simplistic view. When they look deeper at the causes of economic success, they acknowledge – as many contemporary philosophers are loath to do – the substantial role that *luck* plays in the accumulation of wealth and the problems that causes for traditional justifications of moral responsibility and just deserts. Milton Friedman recognizes that *if* we look deep enough, we will find that luck plays a significant role: "Most differences in status or position can be regarded as the product of chance at a far enough remove. The man who is hardworking and thrifty is to be regarded as 'deserving'; yet these qualities owe much to the genes he was fortunate (or unfortunate?) enough to inherit." (1980, 165–66) Contemporary neoliberals deal with the luck problem the same way Fischer does: don't look deep; focus instead on "playing the cards that are dealt us" (Fischer) or investing the resources one currently controls (Friedman). Friedman's basic "ethical principle that would directly justify the distribution of income in a free society" is simple: "to each according to what he and the instruments he owns produces" (1962, 162). Don't inquire about the source of your cards or your investment capital. Contemporary neoliberal theorists (as opposed to contemporary neoliberal politicians) do not claim that those successful in the free market are paragons of traditional virtue, in the sense of being wise and honest and having great fortitude. But differences in wealth are still *just*. Focus on the results produced by one's own abilities and resources when invested in the free market: *that* is the standard for justice. The distribution is a just *process*: the market determines the winners in a process that maximizes efficiency and preserves and promotes liberty. The results – positive or negative – justly accrue to the investor, and that process establishes fairness and justice. Rather than claiming that wealth is gained due to the virtuous qualities of the wealthy, the free market is the *sole* standard for justice.

John Calvin objected to describing God as good or just, because God is the standard for goodness and justice: "God is good" implies that there is a standard of goodness independent of God (a standard to which God must conform). In similar fashion, contemporary neoliberals say that there can be no standard for justice and fairness that trumps the judgment of the *free market*. No matter how you accumulated your starting abilities and starting capital, when you successfully invest them in the free market the benefits you gain belong to you and no one else. The free market passes its positive judgment, individual liberty is preserved, wealth is maximized, and justice is served. Those who work hard may suffer economic failure, while the idle rich become richer. The final judgment of the free market condemns the former and commends the latter. If the invisible hand of the free market can transmute selfishness into virtue, it should not be surprising that it has the power to transform our traditional moral judgments. When neoliberalism is packaged for mass consumption – by politicians and lobbyists and public relations firms – it takes advantage of the ambiguity of neoliberal free market "justice" and combines both traditional and market justice into an attractive package: the *objective* and unbiased free market marks the wealthy as virtuous, *and* the wealthy are the honest, industrious, creative and benevolent "job creators" who justly deserve their enormous wealth.

Attempts to establish moral responsibility come in many shapes and sizes, but they all share an essential feature: they must find a way to make "the buck stop here" and block deeper inquiry. Blocking close examination of deeper causes is essential for preserving just deserts and moral responsibility, and just deserts are essential for justifying neoliberalism. The necessity to block deeper inquiry is also recognized by those eager to incite harsh punitive attitudes and is part of the explanation for why neoliberalism is commonly allied with a harsh "law and order" approach to criminal behavior. As Ronald Reagan recognized, if we "stray" into deep rigorous examination of *why* a person's character and behavior are what they are, then moral responsibility is fatally challenged. The neoliberal British Prime Minister John Major echoed Reagan when demanding harsher punishment for juvenile crime, making clear the essential myopic condition for sustaining belief in moral responsibility and justly deserved harsh punishment: "Society needs to condemn a little more and understand a little less" (quoted in Holborow 1993, 8).

To make the gross inequities and harsh policies of neoliberalism seem fair and just requires a remarkable and implausible doctrine, and moral responsibility is precisely such a doctrine. It is an essential prop for belief in a just world, and the need for moral responsibility becomes even more acute when the task is making the world of neoliberalism appear just. In a profoundly neoliberal culture like the United States, individual moral responsibility is the doctrine that promotes and preserves rugged individualism, extreme economic inequity, and a massive system of harsh criminal punishment.

America is the "land of the free," and all Americans have the opportunity by their own free choices to achieve success: that is a cornerstone of the American myth, a myth that from the founders to the present has justified harsh punishment and poverty alongside wealth and privilege. "The bottom line is that Americans feel that their society offers more chances for everybody to become rich, and those that do not take the chance are lazy and do not deserve much support" (Alesina and Glaeser 2004, 62). The more special the country as the "land of opportunity," the more vile those who fail under such advantageous circumstances. American neoliberalism is deeply committed to individual moral responsibility. The individual is morally responsible for his or her own choices and actions and character, and justly deserves the sweet or bitter fruits of those free choices. When freedom is combined with free will – and both concepts are left vague – then "freedom" serves a special purpose for neoliberals: it provides the foundation for moral responsibility, and moral responsibility justifies not only punishment but also wealth and privilege. The combination of freedom and personal responsibility is celebrated as the basis of our special individual *human dignity*: a human dignity that is preserved and protected by justly deserved punishment and poverty.

7

NEOLIBERAL DIGNITY

Advocates of individual moral responsibility claim that those who are *morally responsible* have a special *dignity* that sets them apart from animals and guarantees their special status as members of the human community. This uniquely human dignity often serves as a consolation prize for those who finish among the losers in the race for success: they may be miserable failures, but so long as they are acknowledged to have made their own decisions and are morally responsible for the outcomes, they at least have their dignity as persons with special powers of free will. They may be economic and moral failures, and they may justly deserve punishment and moral opprobrium, but they are not reduced to objects or animals.

The elite have long used "human dignity" as a charm to justify the mistreatment of the less fortunate, so perhaps it is not surprising that when the appeal to human dignity is challenged – challenged by those who insist on looking deeper into the causes of success and failure – the challengers are portrayed as elitists who are denying the dignity of the less fortunate. Michael Moore is a dedicated advocate of "just deserts" for wrongdoers, and he condemns as elitist anyone who raises questions concerning the deeper causes of criminal behavior:

> In the case of those feelings of sympathy on which the causal theorist relies, one aspect of their psychology should make us hesitate to honour them as sources of moral insight. There is an elitism and a condescension often (and perhaps invariably) connected with such feelings. To stand back and to refuse to judge because one understands the causes of criminal behavior is to elevate one's self over the unhappy deviant. The elevation of self takes place because these causal theorists typically

DOI: 10.4324/9781003284680-7

> maintain high moral standards for themselves, yet refuse to judge others by those same standards. This discrimination betokens a refusal to acknowledge the equal moral dignity of others. It betokens a sense about one's self – as the seat of subjective will and responsibility – that one refuses to acknowledge in others.
>
> *(1997, 545–46)*

Those who seek to discover the causes of criminal behavior are elitists who deny "the equal moral dignity of others." But the only "dignity" denied is the spurious dignity of being a miraculous *causa sui* who transcends all causal history; and that "dignity" is denied for everyone, including both criminals and those who seek to understand the causes of all behavior. Recognizing that we are *all* shaped by causes we did not choose or control is neither condescending nor elitist. Supposing that I deserve full credit for my success and that those who are less fortunate deserve full blame is a justification of elitism, while understanding deeper causes threatens the inequitable "just deserts" claimed by privileged elitists.

Moore makes a similar claim using the troubling case of Richard Herrin. Herrin was a Latino student who grew up in the barrios of Los Angeles and was given financial aid to attend Yale University. While at Yale, Herrin had a romantic encounter with a Yale girlfriend who introduced him to an almost unimaginable life of wealth and luxury. Shattered when she ended their romance, Herrin murdered her. Moore harshly criticizes those who seek to understand the causes of Herrin's terrible act and who question whether Herrin justly deserves severe retributive punishment:

> We are probably not persons who grew up in the barrio of East Los Angeles, or who found Yale an alien and disconcerting culture. In any case, we certainly have never been subject to the exact same stresses and motivations as Richard Herrin. Therefore, it may be tempting to withhold from Richard the benefit each of us gives himself or herself: the benefit of being the subjective seat of a will that, although caused, is nonetheless capable of both choice and responsibility.
>
> Such discrimination is a temptation to be resisted, because it is no virtue. It is elitist and condescending toward others not to grant them the same responsibility and desert you grant to yourself. . . . Herrin had no excuses the rest of us could not come up with in terms of various causes for our choices. To refuse to grant him the same responsibility and desert as you would grant yourself is . . . a refusal to admit that the rest of humanity shares with us that which makes us most distinctively human, our capacity to will and reason – and thus to be and do evil. Far from evincing fellow-feeling and the allowing of others to participate in our moral life,

> it excludes them as less than persons. Rather than succumbing to this elitism masquerading as egalitarianism, we should ask ourselves what Herrin deserves by asking what *we* would deserve had we done such an act.
>
> *(1997, 148–149)*

First, those who look hard and deep at the complex causes for character and behavior do grant others "the same responsibility and desert" they grant themselves: none. Herrin joins *all* of us in the category of persons who do *not* justly deserve punishment. Richard Herrin committed a terrible crime, and attempting to understand the causes of his terrible behavior does not change that fact; but when we look harder at the causes that shape all our behavior, that inquiry challenges belief in just deserts and moral responsibility. We – together with Herrin – have the "capacity to will and reason." But it is not a miracle-working capacity that transcends our causal histories and that everyone shares equally: it varies widely among those who qualify as competent and are able to deliberate and plan.

The just deserts system assumes that all people are *morally responsible* for their behavior unless they have a special excuse. Starting from that assumption, the denial that Richard Herrin justly deserves retributive punishment implies that Herrin is a *special case*, so severely defective that he is excluded from the human moral community. Moore claims that "Herrin has no excuse the rest of us could not come up with in terms of various causes for our choices," but the issue is *causes* rather than excuses. Each of us has a unique causal history, and ultimately none of us chose or controlled the causes that shaped us. Unless we are *causa sui* deities, there are *different causes* in our histories that resulted in our different characters and choices.

Alyssa is a chronic cognizer, who has a powerful sense of cognitive self-efficacy as well as great fortitude and willpower (shaped at a tender age); and Alyssa had superb educational opportunities, was never exposed to environmental toxins, and enjoyed a peaceful and loving childhood. Ben is a cognitive miser who has little confidence in his own cognitive powers, had inferior educational opportunities, was exposed to lead and other toxins that compromised his cognitive capacities and weakened his powers of self-control and damaged his health, and he suffered repeated abuse as well as exposure to traumatizing violence. Both Alyssa and Ben meet the conditions for basic competence: they can think and plan and make choices. But ignoring the enormous differences in their abilities is a form of moral myopia, if not moral blindness. That is the price one pays for clinging to belief in moral responsibility and just deserts, which survives only by avoiding deeper study of the causes that shaped us and that we did not choose or control.

Patty Hearst – a college student who participated in a bank robbery after being violently kidnaped, isolated, and brainwashed – experienced a traumatic period of fear and helplessness for which her wealthy and protected background had left her thoroughly unprepared and with few resources for resistance. Moore insists that her history is irrelevant, and she justly deserves imprisonment for her criminal behavior:

> In the most famous recent example [of brainwashing], the Patty Hearst case, we were certain of a causal connection between the conditioning Hearst received and her criminal behavior. That certainty, however, was irrelevant to the issue of whether her behaviour was an action. She robbed the bank; it was her act, whether or not a situation that was not of her making implanted in her the beliefs that caused her to act. One might have allowed her some affirmative defence if she had not had adequate time between the conditioning and the criminal act in which to reject or integrate her new beliefs into her character. Such an affirmative defence is irrelevant to the issue of action. She plainly acted, whether or not her act was caused.
>
> *(1997, 533–534)*

Moore's claim is not so much false as absurd. It implies that after brainwashing one can "stand apart" from one's newly conditioned character and make an evaluation of whether to "reject or integrate her new beliefs into her character," as if there were some transcendent special platform from which one can evaluate one's character, feelings, beliefs, and reasons from an independent godlike perspective that is sublimely isolated from the traumatic conditions she had experienced and independent of "her new beliefs." If there is someone on that disembodied transcendent platform, it is not Patty Hearst. All of us – including those whose limited capacities for reasoning and self-control are enough to qualify them as *competent* – were shaped by forces we did not choose or control, and those forces varied greatly: ranging from a loving and protective to a violently abusive family, from a healthy and nourishing environment to extensive exposure to harmful toxins, from a social environment that encouraged and rewarded self-control and cognitive effort and inquisitive exploration to the stifling opposite.

Like Moore, Stephen Morse insists that by treating all minimally competent criminals as equal – and studiously ignoring any differences in their histories, conditions, and abilities – we show greater respect for human *dignity*:

> The differences that exist between offenders convicted of the same crime are morally insignificant compared to the similarities. The great value of this position, placing the burden of persuasion on those who believe it is hard to obey the law, is that it treats people with greater respect and dignity than the opposing view, which treats them as helpless puppets buffeted by forces that rob them of responsibility for their deeds.
>
> *(1984, 31–32)*

Those *similarities* that Morse endorses include the one vital characteristic they share: a godlike free will that can rise above all past causes and makes the past irrelevant. Those who *universally* deny moral responsibility do not treat either the virtuous or the vicious as "helpless puppets," but they do insist that considering the extraordinary range of biosocial forces that influence all of us is essential to understanding human behavior.

Perhaps gods have the power to transcend all causal history and act with perfect reason and unlimited willpower; human animals do not. Recognizing this does not imply an "elitist and condescending" attitude toward anyone unless recognizing that humans are mortals rather than deities is disrespectful. Studying and understanding the causes of our behavior, both virtuous and vicious, is a positive step. Blocking such study to preserve moral responsibility and righteous retribution does not promote human dignity. Anyone who cares about promoting and protecting dignity should be cleaning up the environmental toxins that compromise self-control and cognitive powers, providing excellent early education, protecting from abuse, making sure that children have excellent health care and nutrition, and studying and improving the multitude of biosocial factors (Raine 2013) that enhance or compromise abilities and prospects and genuine dignity. Instead, those factors are ignored – or even exacerbated – and "dignity" is provided when the foreseeable result of such neglect is criminal behavior, which is the total responsibility of the individual: an individual whose dignity is now honored by blaming, condemning, and locking him in a cage. This "dignity" is a sham that protects privilege and "justifies" poverty.

Submission to the "will of the market" leaves many people poor and powerless, but they still have their freedom and dignity. If the wealthy are to claim full credit for their wealth (without any consideration of the advantages they had, which would raise questions of their just deserts) then the same principle must apply to the poor: in neither case does the causal history make any difference whatsoever. Everything was open to everyone, everyone has reason and willpower and opportunity, and it's your own fault if you are poor and your own achievement if you are wealthy, and all receive their just deserts.

The Exceptional US Justice System

The neoliberal system combines extreme individualism, just deserts, and market-based moral values. The result is contempt for the poor and harsh punishment for offenders, with "dignity" as a consolation prize. That special "dignity" is obvious in the US justice system.

There are many ways that the US justice system is exceptionally harsh, but the continuing practice of capital punishment is notorious. Capital punishment primarily occurs in authoritarian countries, and no other Western industrialized country practices capital punishment. It was not until 1988

(*Thompson v. Oklahoma*) that the Supreme Court ruled that children could no longer be condemned to death for crimes committed when 15 or younger (Justices Scalia, Rehnquist, and White dissented); the following year (*Stanford v. Kentucky*) the court-approved capital punishment for crimes committed by adolescents aged 16 or 17. Finally, in 2005 (*Roper v. Simmons*), the Supreme Court ruled against all executions for crimes committed by minors. However, the United States continues to execute persons who committed crimes while suffering severe mental illness.

Advocates of the death penalty – and others who promote retributivism – often claim that severe punishment (including execution) shows *respect* for the person punished. C. S. Lewis (a fierce supporter of capital punishment) claimed that: "to be punished, however severely, because we have deserved it, because we 'ought to have known better,' is to be treated as a human person made in God's image" (1971, 246). There may be some world in which execution shows respect for the condemned, but the United States is not such a world. In ancient Greece, citizens (such as Socrates) were given the choice of drinking hemlock; in Rome, citizens were offered the dagger (non-citizens – and slaves – were given no such choice). Citizens were shown respect by having some control over their own deaths (Waller 1989). Under despotic governments, the condemned were often rendered totally helpless during the execution process (British monarchs, eager to show their awesome power over their subjects, executed by the ignominious process of hanging, drawing, and quartering). In the United States, the terrifying power of the state over the condemned is demonstrated by totally immobilizing the prisoner on a gurney while he or she awaits death in a terror heightened by extreme helplessness. When Daniel Lewis Lee was executed – in the middle of the night, July 14, 2021 – he was kept strapped to the gurney for four hours preceding his execution. Any effort by the prisoner to maintain even the slightest degree of control and dignity is zealously blocked. Gary Gilmore, the first person executed following a moratorium on capital punishment in the United States, managed to obtain a supply of barbiturates, and a few days before his scheduled execution he attempted suicide. When the attempt was discovered, he was rushed to a hospital and his stomach was pumped; precisely as scheduled, he was strapped to a chair and killed. Those receiving the death penalty are typically impoverished, and they often have lawyers who are underpaid, marginally competent, and sometimes impaired by addiction.

While capital punishment is an obvious element of American exceptionalism, mass imprisonment is even more harmful. In 2019, the United States carried out 22 executions; during the same year, well over two million people were incarcerated. The United States imprisons its citizens at a rate five times the rate in England and Spain; six times the rate in Canada; almost seven times the rate for Austria, Belgium, Italy, and France; eight times the rate of Switzerland; and between nine and twelve times the rates in Germany, Sweden, Denmark, the Netherlands, Finland, and Norway. William Stuntz

(2011, 48) notes that the imprisonment rate for American Blacks is 80% higher than the rate at which Stalin sent Russians to the Gulag. Through its use of cash bail, the United States holds many poor people in jail for months without trial or conviction (only the Philippines uses a similar system).

American neoliberals promote a harsh retributivist "law and order" policy that they insist shows true respect for those who are imprisoned. Michael Moore claims that efforts to understand the causes of criminal behavior "betokens a refusal to acknowledge the equal moral dignity of others" (1997, 546), while harsh punishment – because it is justly deserved – manifests respect. Herbert Morris insists that wrongdoers have a *right* to be punished which honors their "fundamental right to be treated as a person" (1968, 490). Whatever the "moral dignity" myth, in practice it is difficult to find evidence that American prisons honor the "fundamental right to be treated as a person;" on the other hand, it is difficult to avoid evidence that prisoners are treated with disgust, brutality, and destructiveness – and complete lack of respect.

Rather than respecting the cognitive abilities and "personhood" of prisoners, American Supermax prisons follow solitary confinement practices that are not only psychologically cruel but also cause severe and permanent psychological damage (Arrigo and Bullock 2008; Bersot and Arrigo 2010; Casella and Ridgeway 2016; Grassian 2006; Grassian 2008). The European Court of Human Rights condemns such practices as a violation of the basic human right not to be tortured, while Amnesty International (2012) reached the same conclusion concerning Arizona's maximum-security prisons, and the New York City Bar Association (2011) concluded that US supermax prisons violate the constitutional protection against cruel and unusual punishment. If "respect" has any meaning at all, it must forbid practices that cause psychological and cognitive impairment.

The US neoliberal culture treats prisoners as vile contaminants. Dan Kahan supports mass imprisonment as a means of isolating good people from disgusting criminals: "imprisonment removes offenders from our midst, shielding us from their contaminating influence" (Kahan 1998, 1642). Kahan approves of American prisons that demean prisoners:

> Prison . . . does unequivocally evince disgust. . . . By stripping individuals of liberty – a venerated symbol of individual worth in our culture – and by inflicting countless other indignities – from exposure to the view of others when urinating and defecating to rape at the hand of other inmates – prison unambiguously marks the lowness of those we consign to it.
>
> *(1998, 1642)*

James Conway, former superintendent at Attica Correctional Facility in New York, was deeply disturbed when he visited Halden, a maximum-security prison in Norway in which prisoners are treated with respect, given important work responsibilities, and housed in modest but comfortable facilities resembling dorms at US regional colleges. Conway found such respectful treatment of prisoners (treatment that results in a recidivism rate only a fraction of that in the United States) unacceptable:

> Prison is not supposed to be comfortable. Prison is not a comfortable situation. Society is supposed to be comfortable, the inmate has given up his right to be in society by violating laws, by violent crimes, by committing murder, by committing rape. That person shouldn't be coddled, shouldn't be given a situation where we're concerned about how they should feel if someone should walk by their cell and see them on the toilet. Who cares how they feel?
>
> *quoted in Francis 2014*

Not everyone in neoliberal America supports such cruel and demeaning policies, but the violence and sexual abuse in US prisons (Sigler 2006) is widely known, and few neoliberal citizens are disturbed by it.

The neoliberal "respect" for the dignity of prisoners is also indicated by the common American assumption that those who are imprisoned should lose one of the most basic (though often denied) rights of American citizens: the right to vote (Manza and Uggen 2006). While the European Union forbids any member country from denying the imprisoned the right to vote, in the United States, only two states – Vermont and Maine – allow prisoners to vote, while many states permanently deprive anyone convicted of a felony of voting rights: marking them as either temporary or permanent "outsiders" who can have no role in their own government.

Perhaps the most remarkable evidence of lack of respect for prisoners was provided by Jeffrey Tuomala, a neoliberal advocate of harsh punishment (who adds a "Christian" Calvinist flavoring to his joy in seeing prisoners treated cruelly): "We should respond with satisfaction in seeing wickedness punished, not out of vengeance, but out of respect for justice. . . . When law-abiding people see justice done they should rejoice, and the wicked should be terrified" (1995 22, 27). Tuomala recognizes the horrific treatment of anyone sent to an American prison: "There are all sorts of dangers to his person – beatings, homosexual [actually by heterosexuals] rape, increased risk of disease, and even death. There is a loss of privacy and dignity and perhaps the mental torture of an indefinite sentence" (1995, 28). But rather than condemning this destructive and demeaning treatment, Tuomala draws the opposite conclusion: these cruel conditions are justly deserved by the vile prisoners, and because such conditions are probably worse than flogging therefore it is legitimate to restore flogging as a form of punishment.

The United States is also unique in the extensive use of "for profit" private prisons, where prisoners are sources of profit to be managed as cheaply as possible, and where lowering the recidivism rate means cutting the profits that come from repeat customers. Though for-profit prisons are nothing new (they were widely used and extremely profitable during the Jim Crow era in the deep South and in Texas), the current use of private for-profit prisons started in the United States and the United Kingdom when contemporary neoliberalism became dominant in those countries. One motive was avoiding labor unions that support prison workers; another was the overarching neoliberal principle that everything that can possibly be privatized and profit-driven should be. Though other countries (especially Britain) utilize private for-profit prisons, the United States has far more prisoners in such facilities than any other country: approximately 12 times as many prisoners in for-profit prisons as does the United Kingdom, and the United Kingdom has twice as many as any other country (Mason 2013). Neoliberals appear to believe that cutting all educational and rehabilitation programs and extracting as much profit as possible from keeping people incarcerated is a way of showing respect.

Respect for the Innocent

It is not surprising that the neoliberal myth of universal *respect* – including for prisoners – is the opposite of what is followed in practice. But an even more extreme example of that contrast is found in the neoliberal *principle* of protecting the innocent and the neoliberal *practice* of gross disregard of the rights and protections of those *accused* of crime. The National Registry of Exonerations reported 143 exonerations in 2019 – 143 people who spent years (an average of nine years, sometimes much longer) in a US prison for crimes of which they were innocent; and the National Registry recognizes that there are many more exonerations of which they have no record. Even more troubling, the number of people exonerated is at best only a small fraction of those who have been wrongfully convicted. Since 1993 there have been well over 2,000 exonerations, including more than 200 who were sentenced to death. The best estimates are that between 2% and 10% of convictions are mistaken (Loeffler, Hyatt, and Ridgeway 2019) – which means that somewhere between 46,000 and 230,000 Americans have spent many years of their lives wrongfully imprisoned. Yet in the American neoliberal culture, the wrongful conviction of innocent persons does not appear to be a concern: year after year nothing is done to fix the problems that we know result in wrongful convictions. At the top of that list is the problem of *jailhouse informants*: the false testimony of "incentivized informant witnesses" that one study (Garrett 2008) found was the leading cause of wrongful convictions in US capital cases, and that is a key feature in a wide variety of wrongful convictions of the innocent. The severity of the problem has long been obvious (Natapoff 2006; Roth 2016).

A "jailhouse informant" is a prisoner awaiting trial or sentencing, or who is already serving a prison sentence. That prisoner (typically a repeat offender familiar with the people and the operation of the justice system) learns of a case in which a suspect has been arrested, ideally a high-profile case in which evidence is sketchy. The informant contacts the prosecutor and volunteers to share a cell with (or befriend) the suspect and agrees to inform the prosecutor of any incriminating statements made by the suspect – on the condition that the prosecutor's office provides some help to the informant (such as reduced or dropped charges). Both prosecutors and judges know that the informant is lying. As Myrna S. Raeder (2007, 1438) asks: "Is it really arguable that prosecutors do not know that jailhouse informants who repeatedly claim they obtained confessions are likely to be fabricating?" Justice Stephen Trott (of the 9th Circuit) stated what everyone dealing with the corrupt system of jailhouse informants cannot avoid knowing:

> Because of the perverse and mercurial nature of the devils with whom the criminal justice system has chosen to deal, each contract for testimony is fraught with the real peril that the proffered testimony will not be truthful, but simply factually contrived to "get" a target of sufficient interest to induce concessions from the government. Defendants or suspects with nothing to sell sometimes embark on a methodical journey to manufacture evidence and to create something of value, setting up and betraying friends, relatives, and cellmates alike.
>
> *Northern Mariana Islands v. Bowie, 243 F.3d at 1124, 9th Circuit 2001; quoted in Raeder 2007*

In nearly one in five of the many exonerations, a jailhouse informant's perjured testimony contributed to the wrongful conviction; that includes more than twenty people on Death Row who had been convicted by the perjured and purchased testimony of jailhouse informants (Innocence Project 2019). But the US use of jailhouse informants has not been eliminated (though it has been restricted in a few states), and the US Supreme Court (*Kuhlman v. Wilson*) has ruled that there is no problem with prosecutors offering jailhouse informants special favors in exchange for their testimony (so long as the informant *claims* not to have directly solicited information from the suspect). If a defense attorney bribes a witness, that is the criminal act of suborning perjury; but prosecutors can offer bribes of great value – such as dropped charges – and that is legitimate. This ugly process continues for decades while everyone knows that it perverts the course of justice and results in innocent defendants spending years in prison and sometimes facing a sentence of death.

While the use of bribed jailhouse informants is the most blatant abuse, an even larger systemic problem is the adversarial system. In medieval trial by combat, a just God intervened to ensure that justice triumphed. In the neoliberal American just world, the likelihood of achieving justice through the adversarial system is comparable to the odds in medieval trial by combat. The adversarial system of criminal justice is so deeply entrenched that its obvious flaws and profound unfairness are easily overlooked. At its very best, on a level playing field, the adversarial system is a crude instrument for seeking justice. In the vast majority of cases the playing field is far from level, with one side – the prosecution – holding disproportionate power; and then the adversarial system is an abomination. It gives huge advantages to the wealthy and is heavily weighted against the poor and powerless: which explains why it has survived and thrived in neoliberal America. It is hardly surprising that the result is not only false convictions on a heroic scale but also *false confessions* from many of the wrongly accused. The great majority of defendants are poor, and at best they rarely have the resources to pay for expensive legal talent, not to mention investigators and lab work and expert witnesses. The wealthy are in a different category, a different world altogether. They have enormous resources and squads of lawyers to block efforts at prosecuting them, and they work out a "settlement" involving no jail time that often allows the guilty to keep the profits from their destructive behavior. As William Stuntz notes, "In an adversarial justice system, the government can more easily convict a poor and innocent defendant than a rich and innocent one – perhaps more easily than a rich and guilty one" (2008, 47; see also Menkel-Meadow 1996; Findley 2011–12, 912; and Slobogin 2014).

The problems start as soon as a suspect is arrested (or even before: the police are more likely to arrest a member of a minority group). During the interrogation of the suspect, the police can and do make false claims to get a confession: falsely claiming that the suspect's friend is making a deal with the prosecutor that will lay all the blame on this suspect, while the friend walks; or that there are reliable eyewitnesses or videotapes placing the suspect at the scene of the crime; or that if the suspect will just cooperate and confess the interrogator will convince the prosecutor to greatly reduce the charges. Saul M. Kassin gives a harsh but all too accurate assessment of police interrogations, describing the police interrogator as "a salesman, a huckster as thieving and silver-tongued as any man who ever moved used cars or aluminum siding, more so, in fact, when you consider that he's selling long prison terms to customers who have no genuine need for the product" (1997, 222). Lying to suspects is hardly a way of showing them respect or protecting their dignity. Margaret L. Paris sums up the larger harm caused by such deceptive practices: "It harms a society when the officers who enforce its laws behave like the worst used car salesmen" (1997, 831).

If the defendant still refuses to confess bail may be set at a level the defendant cannot afford, and the "presumed innocent" prisoner spends many months in jail awaiting trial. He or she has "the right to an attorney," but cannot afford one, so a public defender overwhelmed by an enormous case load is assigned the case. Sitting in jail, the accused has no opportunity to seek evidence or work with a lawyer to prepare a defense. The unfair adversarial contest is not confined to the courtroom, but also operates in plea bargaining:

the process that resolves more than 95% of criminal prosecutions (Gramlich 2019), and where the adversarial advantage of the prosecutor is overwhelming. Eventually, an assistant prosecutor, the accused, and the public defender sit down together and the prosecutor makes a one-time offer, take it or leave it. The prosecutor holds all the cards in this "bargaining" process. The overworked public defender has little time to devote to the defendant's case, and even a conscientious defender has not been able to carefully assess the evidence against the defendant (that evidence will not be available until a much later discovery process, in preparation for a trial). The prosecutor has abundant resources, better information, and the powerful threat of very severe charges; the defendant has meager resources, little knowledge of the evidence, no assurance that the information being given by the prosecutor is accurate, no defense against the threat of draconian charges, and is given a "one time offer" that sounds more like a deal offered by an unscrupulous huckster than by an officer of the court.

If the defendant refuses the plea deal and demands his or her "right" to a trial, the prosecutor makes a frightening and genuine threat: if the defendant refuses the deal and goes to trial, the prosecutor will add additional serious charges; and if the defendant is found guilty – as is very likely to happen, given the enormous weight of resources that the prosecution can bring to bear – then the defendant will be serving a much longer prison sentence in an even harsher prison. The prosecutor is referring to the notorious "trial tax": you have a "right" to a trial by jury; but exercising that right comes with a substantial penalty of additional serious charges – and if convicted, much longer prison time (the threat of life imprisonment for three convictions gives prosecutors a very dangerous weapon.) In short, the prosecutor makes them an offer they can't refuse. In a system in which innocent people find it advantageous to plead guilty, it is not surprising that there are many innocent people in prison. An innocent person – who knows well the power of the state to convict – may find it reasonable to confess to the crime. In neoliberal America, it happens every day.

There is one "justice" for the wealthy and a totally different "justice" system of practiced deceit during interrogation, pretrial incarceration for the poor who cannot afford bail, and systemic coercion of guilty pleas for the poor. Why is this blatantly unjust system tolerated in a land of "justice for *all*"? Justice in neoliberal America operates in accordance with the best neoliberal market principles: everyone is entitled to the best justice their money can buy.

8

NEOLIBERAL JUSTICE

The basic structure of neoliberalism is an American constant, not a recent aberration. Neoliberalism waxes and wanes in the United States (it waxed during the Gilded Age and again from the late 20th century to the present, and waned during the New Deal, but it has remained a constant force). Deep belief in a just world (and an exceptionally just country) is supported by moral responsibility and just deserts, and it is combined with rugged individualism, commitment to class differences, reverence for property rights, and systemic racism. The result is harshly punitive criminal justice policies that have continued from the Founders to the present.

Individual moral responsibility legitimizes the wealth of the privileged, validates the reluctance of the wealthy to aid the unfortunate (such aid would interfere with the poverty they justly suffer), focuses blame on the individual disadvantaged wrongdoer, and distracts attention from the deeper causes of wrongful behavior. If the elite are totally responsible for their success, the poor must bear total responsibility for their failure. The same moral responsibility that makes you morally responsible for economic success or failure also makes you morally responsible for your criminal behavior. The roots of this retributive approach to criminal justice are deep, but it flowers in contemporary neoliberalism.

Those who fail in the market or refuse to submit to the market – or to their betters, as judged by market success – justly deserve punishment: whether slaves who rebel against their masters, farmers who cannot pay their taxes and their debts, or anyone who is justly suffering poverty. Those *lacking* property and privilege are sorely tempted to meddle with the judgment of the market and attempt to claim benefits to which they are not entitled. Powerful force is required to compel their submission to the proper order.

DOI: 10.4324/9781003284680-8

The same individual moral responsibility that discourages commitment to helping those who are economically harmed also encourages harsh treatment of offenders: they are isolated individual offenders who are not connected to us – and often seem alien to us – and are not bonded with us by shared social commitments. Cavadino and Dignan offer this description of the contrast between neoliberal individualistic societies and social-democratic cultures:

> Corporatist and social democratic states tend to pursue more inclusionary economic and social policies that offer their citizens a far greater degree of protection against the vicissitudes of market forces, binding citizens to the state via national interest groups and ensuring the provision of welfare benefits and care of various kinds to ensure that all citizens are looked after. The communitarian ethos which gives rise to these policies – and which is in return shaped by them – also finds expression in a less individualistic attitude toward the offender, who is regarded not as an isolated culpable individual who must be rejected and excluded from law-abiding society, but as a social being who should still be included in society but who needs rehabilitation and *resocialization*, which is the responsibility of the community as a whole. The corporate citizen, unlike the neo-liberal, is much more his brother's keeper – even if he has done wrong – with a stronger sense that 'there but for the grace of God go I' – in terms of both economic failure and criminal activity.
>
> *(2006, 448)*

Special powers of free will are the basic justification for moral responsibility and just deserts and righteous retribution, and free will is a license to ignore as irrelevant the harsh inequities and the social and biological environmental burdens that promote criminal behavior. We preserve belief in moral responsibility and justly deserved punishment by scrupulously avoiding examination of the deeper causes, and that willful ignorance of deeper causes precludes discovering and implementing effective measures to prevent and reform criminal behavior.

The deep American commitment to self-made individualism combines with the restraints on inquiry required to preserve moral responsibility, and together they block better understanding of the causes of behavior. When criminal behavior is treated as a freely willed *choice* with no causal antecedents, then criminal behavior is mysterious and inexplicable, and the criminal becomes a strange and frightening creature. There is little sympathy, much less empathy, for dangerous alien criminals so radically different from ourselves, and we are more willing to impose harsh punishment on such monsters (Christie 1993). When dealing with such evil, efforts at rehabilitation seem hopeless: we welcome the view that "nothing works" (Martinson 1974) and that the only solution is long-term confinement (Wilson 1998).

In contrast, careful consideration of the deeper causes for criminal behavior reduces the desire for severe punishment (Doob and Roberts 1983; Fishkin 1992; Indermaur et al. 2012; Indermaur and Roberts 2005; Mackenzie et al. 2014; Pickard 2011; Roberts and Indermaur 2007; Spiranovic, Roberts, and Indermaur 2012). If we want to blame and condemn and punish severely, we must block deeper consideration of the causes of behavior.

In a land of liberty and opportunity, Americans have the special free will that enables them to *choose* the path to prosperity no matter their starting points or backgrounds. Likewise, it doesn't matter whether you were born in poverty or luxury, your economic *failure* is the product of your own free bad choices, and you justly deserve all the blame: the free market doesn't play favorites, and its judgments are final. The same factors that make you totally responsible for your wealth or destitution – exercising your powers of free will in a uniquely free country – also make you individually morally responsible for your honorable or criminal acts. With all the advantages of freedom and free will, anyone who commits a crime had opportunities to take a different and decent path, and that criminal justly deserves full blame and punishment for the crime.

As Thomas Lemke writes, neoliberals:

> distance themselves from all psychological, biological or anthropological explanations of crime. In the opinion of the neo-liberals, a criminal is not a psychologically deficient person or a biological degenerate, but a person like any other. The criminal is a rational-economic individual who invests, expects a certain profit and risks making a loss. . . . However pathological an individual may be, in the eyes of the neo-liberals he or she is always to a certain degree also a rational being, in other words sensitive to changes in the balance of profit and loss.
>
> *(2001, 199)*

Neoliberal dogma notwithstanding, it is ludicrous to suppose that *rational* criminals will calculate that when the penalties increase the risks become too high. The ghetto youth with no opportunities does not rationally deliberate the benefits of gang membership and drug dealing; nor does the member of Congress who engages in fraud, or insider trading. In neoliberalism, the rational man possesses a rationality that transcends all distracting causes or influences, and his rational powers are the godlike rational powers that provide him with the super free will that justifies moral responsibility and just deserts. This attribution of godlike powers of reason to everyone – including criminals – is not a means of showing respect for criminals, but a justification for ignoring the biosocial factors (Raine 2013) that shaped them while imposing the harsh punishment they justly deserve.

The neoliberal just deserts retributivist system produces appalling results: imprisonment rates multiple times those of comparable Western industrialized countries, widespread poverty, and the concentration of wealth and power in the hands of a tiny minority (less than 1%) of the population. Such a destructive policy could not survive – and draw support even from those it severely damages – on its own strengths and "virtues;" it has the support of a belief *system* in which moral responsibility retributivism is protected at the center. Every person has the remarkable power of unfettered choice, and that makes each individual totally responsible for the resulting "self-made man." Your history, environment, background, and family are irrelevant: your godlike choice transcends all mundane influences. The special power of free will is strongly linked with support of retributive punishment (Carey and Paulhus 2013, 138). Linking freedom to moral responsibility does the dirty work for neoliberalism. "Real freedom" means taking personal responsibility and suffering (or enjoying) the consequences of your free choices. In this wonderful free country, we don't care what your background is, it's what you accomplish through your own free will choices and efforts that matter, you "made it all yourself," and you justly deserve all the credit or blame.

Debt, Welfare, and Neoliberal Criminal Justice

Neoliberals view economic failure and moral/criminal failure as comparable: in neoliberalism poverty is the result of deep flaws in morally responsible individuals. Debt is regarded with loathing, and defaults on debt fall into the same category as crimes. Given the focus on money and markets in neoliberal cultures, together with the special emphasis from the founders to the present on the importance of enforcing the payment of debts, it is not surprising that there should be significant overlap between debt and punishment in the neoliberal United States. Even so, the extent of that overlap – and the continued existence of imprisonment for debt, long after it was supposedly banned – is noteworthy.

Debtors' prisons were common in the US at the time of the revolution, and they continued well into the 19th century (Peebles 2013). Among prosperous proto-neoliberal Americans, protection of property was an absolute value, and essential to the protection of property was enforcing the payment of debts. Those who could not pay their debts were little better than thieves, taking property to which they had no right. And because wealth was the primary measure of virtue, anyone falling deep into debt was clearly of inferior moral stature. If a farmer could not pay his debt due to a heavy tax burden, or could not pay the tax itself, the farmer justly deserved punishment: debtors' prison was the just consequence of the farmer's intemperance and indolence.

Imprisonment for debt was abolished in 1833, by federal statute. However, "imprisonment for debt" – often equivalent to enslavement – was widely practiced in the deep South during the Jim Crow period (Adamson 1983; Blackmon 2008; Hinton and Cook 2021; Jones 2017; Oshinsky 1997): it preserved the forced labor system that had existed prior to the Civil War and was part of the brutal system to exert control over "free" Blacks. Following the Civil War and emancipation, Southern "Black Codes" were the legal foundation for mass conviction of Black men. Applied exclusively to blacks, they criminalized such "offenses" as loitering, vagrancy, possessing weapons, and breaking curfew, resulting in massive convictions of Black men. Those convicted were then subjected to the "convict lease system," in which prisoners – who must "pay their debt" to society – were leased out to private contractors, primarily to work in mines, on construction of railroads, and on large plantations. The lease owner had absolute control over the prisoners, with no restrictions on how they were treated, fed, or housed. Because there was a ready supply, prisoners could be worked to death in deplorable conditions and then replaced. Brutal methods were employed in controlling prisoners, including the common use of severe flogging (sometimes to death). Black orphaned children and juvenile offenders were also "bought" through the convict lease system. In addition to providing needed labor and controlling the "dangerous" free Blacks, the leases were enormously profitable to the states. Rather than being burdened by the cost of housing and feeding a massive prison population, the prisoner "leases" were sold to private contractors for large sums. When a prisoner's "debt" was fully paid, the prisoner would supposedly be released; but the leaseholder was the sole judge of when that debt was paid. In fact, conditions were so harsh that few prisoners survived long enough for "full payment" to be an issue, most dying within a few years: the annual mortality rate for prisoners building the Greenwood and Augusta Railroad often exceeded 50%, and the mortality rates at other sites were not far behind (Adamson 1983, 566). The convict lease system continued on a large scale well into the 20th century and did not end until 1941.

Sharecropping was another way that "debt" kept people in bondage – both blacks and poor whites – from Reconstruction until well into the 20th century (Meier and Rudwick 1966). Sharecropper farmers rented land from the owner in exchange for a substantial portion of the farmer's crop. The renting farmer was required to make almost all purchases – tools, seeds, food, housing, clothing – from the landowner, at inflated prices. After harvest, the farmer's share of the proceeds often did not cover the farmer's debt to the landowner. The result was a system of debt peonage: the farmer, bound by debt, was compelled to continue working for the landowner until the debt was paid.

Though we tend to think of debtors' prison as a cruel relic of history, in the neoliberal US, there are currently thousands of people who are imprisoned for debt (though it is now passed off as imprisonment for failure to obey a court order). Debtors cannot be imprisoned for failure to pay their debts; but they can be imprisoned for "willful refusal to pay" when a court – usually (Goldberg 2006) a small claims court (favored by debt-collection firms because the standards of evidence are not as rigorous and defendants are rarely represented by counsel) – rules that a debtor has sufficient resources to repay but is "willfully refusing," and the court issues an order requiring payment. Then when the debtor fails to pay, the debtor is ruled in contempt of court and jailed for that offense (*not* for debt). A variation on this debt-collection device (Shephard 2011) is petitioning a judge to require a debtor to appear in court to assist debt-collectors with collecting. When the defendant fails to appear (because of confusion, or short notice, or difficulty in leaving work or finding child care or transportation or whatever), the judge rules in favor of the creditor; and when the debtor fails to appear for a scheduled post-judgment hearing (for the same reasons) he or she is found in contempt of court and jailed. Extracting money by court order and the threat of imprisonment has become an enormous industry, with debt-collection firms buying up billions in delinquent debts and relentlessly pursuing debtors with harsh methods (Holland 2011, 2014; Holland 2016).

A special form of "debt" results in the jailing of large numbers of indigent persons: the widely used "legal financial obligations" that are incurred by those who fall into the clutches of the criminal justice system. These legal financial obligations (LFOs) include fees for being temporarily held in jail, probation and parole fees, and fees for court costs, drug testing, and electronic monitoring. Elizabeth Jones cites the example of a black woman in Ferguson, Missouri, whose minor illegal parking violation brought these results: she "was ultimately arrested twice, spent six days in jail, and paid $550 to the court. After two years of fee payments and court appearances for the citations, she still owed $541 towards her court-assessed fines and fees" (2017, 39). It may seem strange to charge someone a fee for being compelled to wear an electronic monitoring device, but for neoliberals, it is simply another part of the just market. Those who cannot pay these onerous fees – and the high interest for late payments – are jailed or returned to prison. As Dillon Wamsley notes: "The shift toward a user-funded criminal justice system has contributed to cyclical poverty across the US, particularly in low-income African American communities. LFOs continue to follow debtors long after their release, leading to reincarceration and severely curtailed civil, political, and economic liberties" (Wamsley 2019, 261). They don't call it debtors' prison, but the bars are strong and the harm severe.

Debtors are deprecated in neoliberal society, while those who fail to pay their debts are despised and criminalized. But among contemporary neoliberals, the lowest level of neoliberal hell is reserved for welfare recipients. They are not only poor, but they expect their betters to support their indolence and incompetence – *and* they are eager to defraud the system that sustains them. They demand to be given what rightfully belongs to the industrious, and they scheme to pilfer even more. Kaaryn S. Gustafson provides a clear but depressing picture of the contemporary American neoliberal welfare system:

> Today's welfare system treats those who use public benefits, or even apply for benefits, as latent criminals. Nationwide, welfare recipients are treated

> as presumptive liars, cheaters, and thieves. Their lives are heavily surveilled and regulated, not just by the welfare system, but also by the criminal justice system. Changes in public attitudes and government practices have led to what can be described as the criminalization of poverty.
>
> *Gustafson 2011, 1*

Notwithstanding the fact that neoliberal America has the most meager social support system of all the Western industrialized nations, the despised "welfare system" has become a powerful political strawman in American politics. Isolated cases of individuals abusing the system have been falsely represented as standard practice and used to demand cuts in support as well as even harsher enforcement of its byzantine rules. Ronald Reagan exploited the image of the "welfare queen" for political gain:

> Ronald Reagan used the symbol of the "welfare queen" to propel his ideas on limited government and increased crime control. Reagan used references to the welfare queen to portray an image of widespread depravity and criminality among low-income women of color. Despite the inaccuracies of Reagan's descriptions, the symbol of the welfare queen resonated with the public.
>
> *Gustafson 2009, 653*

The image "resonated" with a neoliberal public strongly inclined to see poverty, depravity, and criminality as a natural combination.

As Gustafson notes, there is substantial "overlap between the welfare system and the criminal justice system," particularly involving "aggressive investigations of and prosecutions for welfare fraud" (2011, 2). But it is not poor welfare recipients who are the major welfare cheaters; instead, the "greatest cheaters" are "doctors and pharmacists and other providers of services who overbill the government" (Babcock and Tyler 1981, A1). But those cheaters are wealthy members of the privileged class, and morally upstanding: the moral problem must center on the poor. The contrast between the assiduous prosecution of small-time welfare "cheats" and the easy acceptance of massive tax fraud (Guyton et al. 2021) by the wealthiest Americans (who are estimated to hide some 20% of their incomes, amounting to roughly $175 billion of tax fraud yearly) is striking, but not surprising in a neoliberal culture. In proto-neoliberal culture, no one was prosecuted – and apparently not even condemned – for using "insider knowledge" to buy up scrip at bargain prices and then cash in when it was paid at full value; but the poor farmers who could not pay the onerous tax which covered the cost of paying for scrip were treated harshly, lost their farms, and were sent to debtors' prison. The American criminalization of the poor and valorization of the wealthy is not a new phenomenon.

Race, Class, and Crime

Blacks in the United States have a shared history of cruel racial abuse and a shared present of racist experience, of being followed by security in upscale stores, targeted by police stops, discriminated against in employment and housing and mortgages. But like whites, blacks are also influenced by class differences, and those differences are apparent in attitudes toward crime and policing. When confronted with rising crime rates and the increasing presence of dangerous illegal drugs, the black professional community (including mayors and other elected officials) and other members of the upper class tend to favor tough law-and-order solutions, including severe criminal sentences; in contrast, local activists and community groups are more likely to support solutions that are nonpunitive and focus on therapy and jobs programs (Forman 2017). That does not mean that class differences trump the shared experience of racial discrimination, but it does indicate the challenges for any effort to draw accurate conclusions concerning racism and classism in neoliberal American culture. Elite universities now admit wealthy blacks who attend expensive prep schools and whose families make large donations to the universities and can afford the outrageous costs. The universities express great pride in their "more diverse" student bodies, which have indeed become more diverse as more blacks have reached the higher echelons of wealth and their children are attending expensive elite prep schools. They are more racially diverse – but with no greater class diversity.

There is no doubt that neoliberalism downplays the influence of racism in American culture. The focus on the operations of a free market and "its rhetoric of individual responsibility serve to justify the *racially* disparate outcomes of the carceral state in *nonracial* terms" (Jones 2017, 43). Don't blame racism for the disproportionate number of blacks who are imprisoned or for the severely disadvantaged economic situation facing blacks; those are the results of an objective free market and the free choices of morally responsible individuals. But while neoliberalism obscures the influence of racism (and in some ways justifies the *results* of racism), the question remains of whether neoliberalism *promotes* racism.

Neoliberalism – from the beginning to the present – is strongly classist; is it also racist? Because in the US class and race are so deeply entangled that is a difficult question to answer. The harsh history of racism has resulted in a disproportionate number of blacks living in poverty and relatively few among the wealthy and privileged. Neoliberalism denigrates the poor, and in a racist society that results in mistreating a disproportionate number of blacks because blacks are disproportionately impoverished. Another complicating factor, especially in contemporary neoliberalism: many of the political backers of neoliberalism have exploited racism to promote their goals. Ronald Reagan's distorted attacks on "welfare queens" were central to his racist campaign strategy, and that is only one example of the comprehensive "Southern strategy" of the strongly neoliberal Republican Party in the late 20th century. But it is not clear that there is something distinctive about neoliberalism that links it to racism. The proto-neoliberal founding fathers were profoundly racist; but while their deep devotion to property (including the property of slaves) exacerbated the racism, it is quite likely that their deep racism would have persisted no matter what their views of the market.

Americans cherish Abraham Lincoln's stirring claim that America was "conceived in liberty, and dedicated to the proposition that all men are created equal." The truth is very different. At its conception America was a nation of slavery, many of the Founding Fathers were slave owners, and even those who were opposed to slavery were more dedicated to protecting property than ending slavery. Slaves were property, and if that property escaped it had to be returned to its rightful owner; and if slavery was to be ended, then slave-owners must be compensated for the loss of their property. And America was certainly *not* "dedicated to the proposition that all men are created equal." Obviously, slaves were not considered equals, and citizens with little or no property were not allowed to vote or hold office. "Liberty" meant one thing when exalted by the founding elite, and something quite different when applied to slaves and the poor. America is deeply rooted in inequality.

Slavery had a powerful impact on the obsessive protection of "property" rights in the United States and was also an important factor in promoting and maintaining the exceptionally harsh system of "justly deserved" punishment. Slavery remained legal in the United States for many years after it had been banned in Europe and the United Kingdom, and it was practiced on an enormous industrial scale on cotton, rice, and sugar cane plantations. The long history of slavery – with its torture, mutilations, brutal punishments, and terrorist methods to instill fear and hopelessness and prevent escapes and uprisings – was one factor in the harsh history of American "justice." To keep large numbers of strong men and women in bondage – men and women who knew full well that they had no possibility of better conditions so long as they remained enslaved – extremely cruel measures were adopted, including common use of torture. Slave owners could do as they wished with their property, and that made torture "just." The brutal practice of "just punishment" toward slaves inevitably seeped into the larger standards of just punishment: any threat to property and wealth could be punished very harshly, including by execution. Theft of a horse or other property in the West was subject to "swift justice" at the end of a rope. And if some innocent people were wrongly executed – well, they were poor, and therefore probably guilty of something. The important thing was that someone had to suffer for any attack on the sacredness of property.

After the abolition of slavery, the brutal control of former slaves – during the decades of the Jim Crow era – employed the same terrorist methods that had been honed during legal slavery, adding widespread lynching to the tortures used to control slaves. Many innocent people spent their miserable lives on prison farms and laboring in "convict lease" industries that were no better and probably worse than slavery (Oshinsky 1996; Mancini 1996; Blackmon 2008). Many were on chain gangs for the egregious crime of "not knowing their place." All this repressive machinery played its part in producing a criminal justice system with little regard for the truth, less regard for the rights of the accused, and no concern for horrific punishments. The cruel and unjust activities of the Jim Crow era were well-known throughout the country, but they were more often celebrated – in films such as "The Birth of a Nation" and "Gone with the Wind" – than deplored; and they continued for a full century after supposed "emancipation."

The long legacy of slavery and deeply entrenched racism has played a powerful part in the exceptionally cruel and unjust "system of justice" in the United States (Acharya, Blackwell, and Sen 2016). Belief in a Just World (BJW) exerts a powerful but subtle and typically nonconscious influence, inclining us to believe that the world is justly ordered and that the existing state of the world is just. When the relevant "world" is a country of exemplary justice and virtue (a country blessed and favored by a just God), then the belief gains an even stronger hold. Moral responsibility preserves BJW by transforming victims of injustice into villains who are getting what they justly deserve. When the evidence of injustice is powerful, the belief in moral responsibility must be robust. The wickedness of the *apparent* victim of injustice must correspond to the level of justly deserved suffering. This might be called "The Fundamental Law of BJW": the more severe the injustice, the more vile the victim. Those we subject to torture are terrorists. The indigenous peoples who are murdered, displaced, and confined on reservations are bloodthirsty savages. And those of African descent who for centuries are enslaved, subjected to Jim Crow terrorism, discriminated against, harassed, and imprisoned must be persons of exceptional depravity who are suffering their just deserts: the horrific wrongs perpetuated against black victims require that blacks be portrayed as exceptionally evil and dangerous. The more unjustly we treat people the more we must convince ourselves that they justly deserve such treatment in our just world. The relation of racism to neoliberalism is complex but powerful.

9

THE NEOLIBERAL ACADEMY

Education is represented as the great equalizer. From the founders to the present, it has been the great preserver of elitism. The founders set property requirements for voting and holding office, not education requirements; but that was because property was and is the supreme value, and education was its handmaiden. Only the elite went to college, with the planters sending their sons north to become educated and enhance their elite status. There was an effort to provide universal basic education, and some "red brick" state colleges were built for the middle class, but the elite colleges were almost exclusively for the elite and confirmed their elite quality. In the late 20th century, the desire for an elite education became an obsession. A college education became common, and desirable; but an *elite* college education was the real mark of success and a guarantee of the continuing elite status of the family.

Meritocracy is a powerful American myth. Like liberty and justice for all, America is a land of opportunity, a true meritocracy where success is open to all, and the elite are those who rise to the top on their own efforts and merits. The meritocracy myth is centered on wealth, the wealthy are the best and brightest, and through their creative efforts, they are the "job creators" who make the economy work for the greatest possible benefit. Education supports the meritocracy myth in two important ways. Part of the special merit of the elite is their superior education ("superior education" is measured by the elite quality of the educational institutions attended, from prep schools to Ivy League universities). And second, educational opportunity legitimizes the *merit*-based system. Education is the stairway – open to all – to the elite heights. Everyone can work hard, study hard, and reach the top no matter where he or she started. That is a key element of the neoliberal myth, spread

DOI: 10.4324/9781003284680-9

through Horatio Alger stories, the popular press, the hopes of youth, and the testimony of the wealthy elite. The neoliberal reality is a different story.

Education is not the great equalizer, but instead a major factor in maintaining an extreme class hierarchy. The Founding Fathers and original framers – who made their distaste for democracy and the masses quite clear when talking among themselves – were an economic and educational elite, they were certain that their elite status was justly deserved, and they were devoted to maintaining the power and control and position of the educated elite. Their wealth and the power and influence of their family connections made them elite, but their "superior educations" were their own doing and established their justly deserved positions among the privileged.

While literacy was widespread, for many decades college educations were rare in the United States: there were few colleges, they were largely reserved for "gentlemen's sons," and in any case, only "gentlemen" could afford to send their sons to college. As the number of people attending college increased – especially in the second half of the twentieth century – a college education was no longer a reliable marker for distinguishing the elite from the masses, but the US education system rose to the challenge of elite preservation. Almost anyone could go to college, but a few elite universities were reserved for the wealthy and well-connected. A degree from Western Michigan or the University of Georgia was fine, and was usually a ticket to middle-class security; but a degree from Harvard or Yale marked one as not only one of the elite but as one whose superior education – gained by his or her own superior abilities – justified a place at the top of the meritocracy, and the superior educational efforts and achievements of the elite made it obvious that their wealth and power were their *just deserts*. Michael Young makes clear the effects of this elite education-based sense of meritocracy:

> The business meritocracy is in vogue. If meritocrats believe, as more and more of them are encouraged to, that their advancement comes from their own merits, they can feel they deserve whatever they can get. They can be insufferably smug, much more so than the people who knew they had achieved advancement not on their own merit but because they were, as somebody's son or daughter, the beneficiaries of nepotism. The newcomers can actually believe they have morality on their side. So assured have the elite become that there is almost no block on the rewards they arrogate to themselves.
>
> *(2001)*

The "merit" established by a degree from one of the elite universities is just as fake as the "meritocracy" established by nepotism; the key difference is that when the ticket to the top of the meritocracy is a degree from an elite university, those at the top may be more likely to believe they "did it all on my own and justly deserve all the benefits" (although the many generations whose top spots in the "meritocracy" were the blatant result of nepotism and inherited privilege rarely had much difficulty convincing themselves that their elite positions were their just deserts). As Amy Liu states:

> conventional wisdom suggests that meritocracy is a positive system in which society functions. Individuals may believe they are deserving of their reward – be it power, authority, status, and/or wealth – because it has been the product of their own talent and effort.
>
> *(2011, 384)*

The meritocracy myth is deeply embedded in the American culture and held in place by strong belief in miraculous *causa sui* powers of free will, the moral responsibility that free will justifies, and the rugged individualism strengthened by the influence of the frontier. That myth prepares the ground for acceptance of the belief that those with degrees from elite universities are entitled to elite positions in the meritocracy. The elite universities have been happy to support that myth and reap the benefits of their privileged status.

The Elite College Admission Scam

Though widely believed, it is false that a degree from an elite university proves that one has exceptional qualities of fortitude, intelligence, or creativity. The strong belief in that false conclusion comes from a variety of sources. First, many believe that admission to Harvard and comparable elite universities is based on a fair competition among high-achieving students, with the best and brightest winning the cherished spots. There were more than 43 thousand applicants for the Harvard class of 2023, and fewer than two thousand – significantly fewer than one out of twenty applicants – were accepted (Caldera and Mohammadzadeh 2019), while many superb applicants were denied admission. There is indeed stiff competition for admission to Harvard, but that competition does not occur on a level playing field.

Harvard boasts of how many valedictorians it turns away (with deep regret, of course), but prefers not to speak of the many mediocre students admitted due to *legacy*. Applicants whose parents or grandparents attended Harvard have a favored *legacy* status that increases their chances of being admitted. If that legacy status is enhanced by substantial (multi-million dollar) financial gifts to Harvard, then the legacy student is placed in a special category – the "Dean's Interest List" – that almost guarantees admission. Some admission officers speak of legacy privileges as being able to heal the sick, not raise the dead; but some of the students who are "healed" had planted at least one academic foot squarely in the grave before their legacy privileges resurrected them. The legacy privilege is not mere tokenism (as is the case for the tiny group of poor students who are admitted and given aid). Legacy applicants are accepted to Harvard at a rate of approximately 34% (and of course the *super* legacy students at a much higher rate). Since the overall acceptance rate is under 5%, and more than a third of those accepted are legacy students, applicants who do *not* have the legacy advantage have an acceptance rate of under 3%.

Admissions departments at elite schools are very reluctant to share data on how many of their students are legacy students,. but Kahlenberg (2010) reported that "almost three-quarters of research universities and virtually all liberal arts colleges grant legacy preferences." That should not be surprising. How do you suppose Harvard accumulated an endowment of 42 billion dollars? The same way that Yale accumulated 30 billion, Stanford 28 billion, and Princeton 26 billion. They proudly proclaim that they give some needy students substantial scholarships; but very few, in contrast to those whose parents pay full tuition and millions in donations. The legacy scam is not widely known and many superb but naive applicants to Harvard are deeply disappointed that they did not "measure up" to Harvard's high standards of admission. Not every elite school gives such favored treatment to "legacy" applicants, but those that do not are exceptions.

Though legacy admissions play a large role in determining who gains entry into the elite universities, a substantial number of applicants win the application game with no help from legacy favoritism. Those are the students who score high on the SAT, do well on a number of Advanced Placement (AP) courses, and can boast of outstanding accomplishments outside the classroom. The case for admission *meritocracy* at the elite universities rests heavily on the measurable accomplishments of those students. But on closer examination, high scores on standardized tests cannot carry the burden of admission meritocracy.

Standardized tests – especially the SAT – have become a major factor in the fight for admission to elite "highly selective" universities. At first glance, such tests may seem a fair measure of academic ability: everyone takes the test and those who score highest win. But a second glance quickly reveals that the competition is far from fair. The most obvious unfairness occurs when wealthy parents pay someone to take the test for their son or daughter; that happens, but it is comparatively rare, and not the major problem. The second obvious problem is that many wealthy students get *extra time*, extra time on tests for which time pressure is a major factor in success or failure. A friendly – and expensive – psychologist diagnoses the student with a "learning disorder" that provides the privileged student with double time. Some students really do need extra time to compensate for special problems, but many wealthy students exploit that loophole to gain a big boost on the "level playing field" that the test is supposed to offer. The third factor that slants the "level playing field" is that wealthy students can afford to take the test many times, even making long trips for that purpose, and then submit their best score. These are obvious problems for the fairness of such tests, but they are still not the most significant problem. The deepest source of unequal opportunity is that wealthy students have access to preparation and training that most students cannot afford. As Amy Liu points out, "a whole industry has developed that persists in undermining equality of opportunity. An entrepreneurial admissions sector comprised of commercial enterprises aimed at helping students increase their odds of admission exists to capitalize on the inevitably unequal distribution of limited spaces" (2011, 390).

SAT prep courses are big business, and the training they offer varies greatly in quality and price. The top courses cost several thousand dollars, and the cost for a tutor may run close to ten thousand dollars or even more. In addition, students at elite prep schools often have special courses that prepare them for the SAT. Tuition and board for a year at one of the most prestigious prep schools are around 55 to 60 thousand dollars, and one of the main reasons parents spend that much is the expectation that when the students graduate, they will have an excellent chance at admission to one of the elite universities; so these elite prep schools devote great effort to preparing their students for the SAT. Crafting each student's application package – making sure they have an impressive mix of extracurricular activities, service projects, the right AP courses – is the work of several years and a staff of experts. Consider the opportunities and guidance (not to mention connections at top universities) offered a student at Exeter or Andover or Groton, compare them with the resources of a rural Appalachian or an urban inner-city high school, and judge whether the test-dominated admissions competition still seems fair.

Even if the SAT competition occurred on a level playing field – which it obviously does not – there would remain a much deeper question: does a high score on the SAT show that a student has the abilities needed for either academic or long-term success? There is a *positive correlation* between high SAT scores and long-term financial success, but that shows nothing about whether the SAT measures special abilities. Because of the grossly uneven playing field, the children of the wealthy score higher on the SAT than do the children of the poor; likewise, the wealthy children are much more likely to be wealthy adults than are the poor children. The former inherit wealth from their parents, and they have family connections that guarantee them high-paying jobs whatever their level of competence. It is true now as it was when Jesus of Nazareth said it some two millennia ago: "To him that hath shall be given; and from him that hath not shall be taken, even that little which he hath." But that does not mean that "him that hath" is better qualified than "him that hath not." The SAT measures how well students have been trained to answer the specific types of questions that appear on the SAT. It does not measure – or even pretend to measure – valuable skills like ability to work cooperatively and productively with a team, leadership skills, inquisitiveness, creativity, or fortitude.

There is an even deeper question about the value of the SAT: does it measure skills for the sort of society we want? And does training students to score well on the SAT enhance the abilities that would make positive contributions to a democratic society? Lani Guinier, Professor at Harvard Law School, characterizes the process of high-stakes admission testing (through instruments like the SAT) as a "testocracy," a type of "meritocracy" that judges individual merit through special tests. She argues that it is a harmful and short-sighted system that promotes values contrary to those that are essential in a democratic society:

> Harvard economist Amartya Sen defines "merit" as an incentive system that rewards the actions a society values. Defining merit through students' grades and test scores is evidence that our society values individual competition above all else. . . . It is now time for another culture shift: from honoring testocratic merit to honoring democratic merit.
>
> *Guinier 2015, xi*

Guinier condemns the "elite-sponsored admissions practices that transform wealth into merit, encourage over-reliance on pseudoscientific measures of excellence, and convert admission into an entitlement without social obligation" (2015, 23). She notes the work of Jo Boaler, a professor of mathematics education at Stanford who developed a highly successful math program at a Bay area high school with a large percentage of low-income students. Boaler's students worked cooperatively at their math studies, and the results were outstanding (even when measured by standardized tests they outperformed students at schools with much more affluent student bodies). But Boaler's goals were larger than producing higher scores on standardized math tests. Boaler argues that our schools should "produce citizens who treat each other with respect, who value the contributions of others with whom they interact, irrespective of their race, class, or gender, and who act with a sense of justice in considering the needs of others in society" (2008, 184).

Training for the SAT is only a small part of the expensive process of maximizing a student's chances of admission to an elite university. The student's "personal statement" is coached and edited – not infrequently to the point of being ghostwritten – by professional writers who charge premium fees for producing essays that will win the favor of admissions officers. Another important consideration for admission to elite universities is the number of advanced placement (AP) courses the student has taken. Wealthy suburban schools typically offer a decent selection of such courses, while top prep schools offer many more along with specialized teachers for each subject. Schools that have fewer resources – the schools attended by poor and lower-middle-class students – offer few if any AP courses.

Admissions committees at elite universities also consider evidence that the applicant is a well-rounded student with wide interests and strong commitments. An excellent way of demonstrating such desirable qualities is through carrying out an impressive service project, ideally in an exotic land. The student "directs" the project, while Mom and Dad hire experts to do the work. It's expensive, but wealthy parents who are driven to get their kids admitted to elite universities are willing to pay. If instead students must spend much of their time working to help their families or to save for college tuition, and they don't have the time for impressive unpaid service projects – well, tough luck. A professional counselor – provided by a prep school or paid directly – walks the wealthy student through all the details and steps and preparation for the application process, and coaches the student on every step. Such highly skilled and highly paid counselors work with students starting in the freshman year of high school, or perhaps earlier, guiding students to take the right courses, perform "service" projects that are most appealing to elite admissions committees, and participate in the right extracurricular activities. Souping up a car that wins trophies at the local drag strip requires hard work and demonstrates substantial technical knowledge as well as fortitude, but it's not likely to enhance your chances of admission to Harvard or Yale. Neither will working long hours at McDonald's to help with the family finances. Being an editor of the school paper is much better; being editor of the generously supported award-winning school paper (with its highly professional faculty advisors providing extensive advice and assistance) at Exeter or Andover is best of all. Diana Kendall notes another "special benefit" of attending an elite prep school: "Most significantly, however, elite private schools convey to students the idea that their privilege is justified" (Kendall 2006, 97; see also Cookson and Persell 1985).

One last obvious obstacle that bars the gates of elite universities to poor and middle-class students: the cost of tuition and board. For parents in the wealthiest 1%, that cost is trivial compared to the cost of several years of prep school, special SAT tutoring, a college admissions advisor, and probably several million in generous donations to the beloved elite *alma mater.* Tuition for Columbia University was approximately $64,000 for 2020–2021; Brown was 58, Yale was 55, Stanford 55, Princeton 53, and Harvard was a bargain at $52,000. Add at least 18 or 20 thousand for room and board – and a few thousand for incidentals such as books – and the annual cost will run at least $75,000 per year. Middle-class families cannot afford such costs; and for families in the lower-income group, the cost for a year at Yale would be more than twice their total income.

A 2017 study of enrollment at 38 elite colleges (Chetty et al. 2017) found that students from families in the top 1% – those with annual income of more than $630,000 – had more students enrolled than the total enrollment of students from families in the bottom 60% (families making less than $65,000 a year); and students from the top 1% are 77 times more likely to be admitted to and attend an Ivy League school than are students coming from families that make less than $30,000 a year. Thomas Piketty makes clear the enormous impact of wealth on access to higher education in the United States, noting that while more than 90 percent of young adults from families in the highest 10% of income attend college, for those from families in the lowest 10% of income the number attending college (including two-year colleges) was approximately 20%. The dramatic difference in college attendance is not the only important factor:

> Access to higher education does not mean the same thing for those at the top and bottom of the distribution. The concentration of educational investment in elitist institutions is particularly extreme in the United States, whose admissions procedures are opaque and public regulation is almost entirely lacking.
>
> These results are striking because they illustrate the wide gap that separates official meritocratic pronouncements (which emphasize – theoretically and rhetorically, at any rate – equality of opportunity) from the realities facing the most disadvantaged students.
>
> *(2020, 34–35)*

Higher education – especially at elite institutions – plays a vital role in the promotion and protection of neoliberalism. It provides the "meritocracy" framework for justifying gross inequity, both by its admission policies and the ideology of just deserts and moral responsibility it promotes:

> In the United States, France, and most other countries, the praise heaped on the meritocratic model is rarely based on close examination of the facts. The goal is usually to justify existing inequalities with no consideration of the sometimes glaring failures of the existing system or of the fact that lower- and middle-class students do not have the same resources or courses as the children of the upper classes.
>
> *Piketty 2020, 712*

Piketty describes the "meritocracy" system with painful clarity: "Today's meritocratic ideology glorifies entrepreneurs and billionaires. At times this glorification seems to know no bounds. Some people seem to believe that Bill Gates, Jeff Bezos, and Mark Zuckerberg single-handedly invented computers, books, and friends" (Piketty 2020, 713).

Legacy admission, testocracy, and high tuition guarantee that the privileged will make up the vast majority of Harvard students. Still, they must be brilliant students if they manage to graduate from Harvard's rigorous educational program: if you made it through the tough academic grinder at Harvard, then no matter how you got in and however you managed to pay for it, that *proves* you are among the best and the brightest. Or so it is widely assumed, but not by those who have any familiarity with academic life at highly selective bastions of privilege such as Harvard and other elite Ivy League Universities. The fact is that once admitted to one of the elite universities, it is more difficult to flunk out than it was to get in. Grade inflation is a concern at many schools, but not in the Ivy League, where the grades are already so inflated they cannot go higher. In 2013, Jay Harris, the former Dean of Undergraduate Education at Harvard, revealed that the median grade at Harvard was an A-minus; the most common grade was A. Few students receive a grade below B plus, no matter the quality of the work. A grade of B is considered a personal assault and is likely to cause the grade-giver considerable grief. Graduate students – who teach many of the courses and assign the grades – are especially vulnerable, and they soon learn that giving grades below the A-level is hazardous to their academic health ("I didn't pay twenty million to this university to have my grandson's chances for law school ruined by some snotty graduate student"). Ivy League students are wealthy, and their families have plenty of money for lawyers and lots of friends in high places and enormous power for causing trouble for anyone – even a tenured professor – who gives their cherished child or grandchild a low grade that might imperil his or her passage to law school or med school or graduate school. Who needs that sort of bother, which will involve angry parents, tearful students, threatening lawyers, and probably a stern rebuke from the Dean? The faculty know they are judged on their research, not on their teaching, and trouble over grades is a big distraction from the research the faculty member wants to pursue. Some faculty find this sham grading process disturbing, and they give their students two grades: the official grade (of A) that will go on their transcripts; and the grade they actually earned, which is given only to the student.

The inflated grades at Harvard and Yale and similar schools are nothing new. Former President George W. Bush attended an elite prep school, Phillips Academy, which smoothed his way into Yale. He entered Yale in 1964 and graduated in 1968. At that time grade inflation was not as extreme as it later became; students whose work was very weak – even awful – received a "gentleman's C." Bush, who played rugby and partied with his fraternity and another social club, graduated with a 2.35 GPA, which included no A grades during the four years. Bush himself stated that he was known for his partying rather than his grades; but he was never in danger of flunking out, no matter how poorly he might have done in his courses. By the time Brett Kavanaugh entered Yale, a "gentleman's C" had become an A-minus. Justice Kavanaugh followed a similar path to Yale, by way of an elite prep school. He attended Georgetown Prep, which currently costs over $60,000 per year. He claims he studied hard. He also partied hard and drank hard. Like all his classmates, he was carefully prepped for admission to the Ivy League and taught all the tricks for improving his application. During his years at Yale, he received excellent grades – hardly anyone received anything else, whether they worked hard or not. During his testimony before the Senate Judiciary Committee, a Senator asked questions about his reputation for heavy drinking during his prep school and Yale years; he responded: "Senator, I was at the top of my class academically, busted my butt in school. Captain of the varsity basketball team. Got in Yale College. When I got into Yale College, got into Yale Law School. Worked my tail off." Perhaps some people were impressed: Yale College and Yale Law, must be brilliant and hard-working. But anyone who knew anything about the "academic rigor" of Yale considered it a joke. Between Georgetown Prep privilege and Yale grading scale, brilliance and diligence had nothing to do with Kavanaugh's "academic achievements." The faculty and administrators played the generously rewarded game at Georgetown Prep and Yale and sent this mediocre thinker and credibly accused sexual predator and heavy drinker to the Supreme Court to defend elite privilege and sham meritocracy and neoliberalism. Both Yale and Georgetown Prep are eager to celebrate their achievement in placing their graduate on the Supreme Court, and they are delighted rather than disturbed by the elitist system they are perpetuating.

A degree from a prestigious and highly selective university does not imply that one has received an outstanding education – especially when we add the consideration that even the weakest and laziest students will receive excellent grades and graduate on schedule, so long as their tuition payments are made. As Rebecca Shamash states: "Rather than implying superior capability or even a more thorough educational experience, these degrees are proof of association with a valuable brand and evidence that an individual is likely to exhibit the type of 'fit' or 'polish' valued by elite professional service firms" (Shamash 2018, 15). The valuable association goes well beyond a "valuable brand." The connections and friendships formed at elite universities are a special ticket into elite jobs after graduation. One study (Marmaros and Sacerdote 2002) of Dartmouth graduates found results that are hardly surprising: a strong positive correlation between obtaining high-paying jobs at elite firms and obtaining help from fraternity and sorority contacts and connections.

Daniel B. Saunders makes clear the profound influence of neoliberalism on American education: "Just as the individuals in the neoliberal world are in constant competition with one another . . . , students in the neoliberal university become less like members of a community of learners and more like individuals focused on enhancing their human capital and who are solely responsible and accountable to themselves" (2010, 63). The "meritocracy" (or "testocracy") that dominates the elite universities and their students exacerbates the radical individualism at the heart of neoliberalism and perpetuates an elite class that exerts power for its own preservation and its own narrow interests. Getting beyond this destructive system requires that we dismantle the myth of meritocracy and confront the powerful factors that result in a grossly unfair playing field as well as the obsessive individualism that undercuts efforts to establish a genuine democracy. When we carefully examine what is needed for a democratic culture that affords real opportunity and liberty and justice for all, it is clear that the values of neoliberalism – and the elitist educational system neoliberalism supports – are fundamentally incompatible with democratic ideals.

Education should be the great leveler of opportunity; it has become the great preserver of privilege. Education should be the great preparation for democracy, something neither two-year colleges nor the most elite universities provide. There can be no "government of the people" if the "people" are easily misled by lies and propaganda. Education for democracy must distinguish the neoliberal myth from economic reality, and the Founding Fathers myth from the racist and elitist and anti-democratic reality, and must challenge the destructive myopic belief in moral responsibility and meritocracy that justifies elite privileges and harms the victims of the neoliberal system.

College, Contempt, and Culture Wars

Elite colleges and unfair admission practices promote and protect an elitist class structure, and that is the source of major problems in our inequitable neoliberal society. But there is a second elitist harm in American higher education, and it is much broader: the arrogance of the college-educated (whether educated at Yale or Ohio State or Northern Arizona) and their contempt toward those who do not have a college education. The result is justified resentment among those who have less education. The larger disastrous outcome is a deep and distrustful cultural divide, the nasty and destructive "culture wars" between the arrogant college-educated and the angry non-college people. Those on one side are condemned as stupid and authoritarian, and they return the compliment: liberals have no respect for tradition and authority, and loyalty. That oversimplifies: there are many who never spent a day in college who are liberal or even radical in their views, while there are multitudes of highly educated who favor the most repulsively narrow and bigoted authoritarianism. But there are broad differences between those who have and those who have not attended college, and those differences are exacerbated by differences in economic class.

College-educated liberals often attempt to hide their contempt, but it shines through the cracks and those without college degrees are painfully alert to its manifestation. The less educated – many of whom are suffering economically and psychologically as they watch others flaunt their wealth and success – are called "deplorables" by Hillary Clinton; and Barack Obama, speaking of small-town midwestern voters, made these unfortunate remarks: "They get bitter, they cling to guns or religion or antipathy to people who aren't like them or anti-immigrant sentiment or anti-trade sentiment as a way to explain their frustrations." This was a half-hearted effort at looking for deeper causes, but the effort was weighted with contempt. If he had said, "They are bitter, and they have damned good reasons to be bitter, and we need to recognize those problems and all work together to fix them," that would have been better; and had he admitted that we – the college-educated and to some degree elite liberals – have largely ignored their problems and have sometimes been the source of those problems, that would have been best.

Thomas Piketty notes how tempting it is to suppose that racism caused the defection of many in the working class from the Democratic Party (with its traditional support for labor) to the Republican Party (with its appeal to racism and xenophobia). But it is a temptation that should be resisted, along with the inadequate explanation it promotes. Piketty contrasts "the nativist hypothesis" (the less advantaged were drawn to the racist and anti-immigrant demagoguery of the Republican Party) with "the social hypothesis" (which he endorses, and which attributes the change to a sense of abandonment felt by the less-educated working class, as the Democratic Party – with its strong emphasis on education – began to draw more support from the better educated). He does not deny the influence of the racist and xenophobic Republican messaging, but he does deny that it is an adequate explanation for the shift of working people away from the Democratic Party:

> There is no denying that in recent decades, nativist, racist, and anti-immigrant themes have been exploited to the hilt by parties of the traditional right . . . . Nevertheless, the nativist hypothesis poses numerous problems and, in my view, fails to give a correct account of the observed changes. The key fact is that the reversal of the educational cleavage is a long-term phenomenon that began in the 1960s and 1970s . . . . It is obviously very convenient for the elites to explain everything by stigmatizing the supposed racism of the less advantaged. However, racism is not more "natural" among the least favored classes than among the well-off.
> *(2020, 754)*

A better explanation is provided by the social hypothesis:

> Briefly put, the social hypothesis is this: that the less educationally advanced classes came to believe that the parties of the left now favor the newly advantaged educated classes and their children over people of more modest backgrounds. . . . The electoral left was transformed from the workers' party into the party of the educated . . . . Indeed, it is easy to understand why those who improved their social status through education and particularly through public schooling would in many ways feel grateful to the parties of the left, which always stressed the importance of education as a means to emancipation and social advancement. The problem is that many who succeeded in this way developed smug and condescending attitudes toward the rest of the population; or, to put it more charitably, they did not inquire too deeply into whether official "meritocratic" pronouncements corresponded to reality or not.
> *(2020, 755–756)*

Rather than the working class abandoning the progressive Democrats in favor of racist demagogues, the Democratic Party abandoned – or made unwelcome through "meritocratic" contempt – the less educated working people, who were then drawn to racist and xenophobic appeals that offered answers and "sympathy" to those who were suffering the pain of economic disadvantage. The racist and xenophobic targets (who are "taking your jobs" and "getting privileged treatment") were blamed in order to obscure the fact that the super-elite were in fact taking massive amounts of money that should have gone to working people, but it was an easy sell to the suffering members of the working class who felt scorned and abandoned by the better educated Democratic Party.

Until we try to understand the causes of crime, we will not deal effectively with crime: the conservatives say that is sympathizing with the murderer. And until we try to understand the causes of racism, we won't deal effectively with racism: some liberals say that is sympathizing with racists. During the white supremacist rally and the counterprotests in Charlottesville, Donald Trump said there were good people on both sides; and so there were. For Trump, racism was one of the virtues of the "good people" who were championing white supremacism; but vile as their beliefs and prejudices are, there *were* some good people on both sides. White supremacism is a terrible thing; but white supremacists aren't inexplicable monsters, any more than murderers are; and racists are not devoid of other character traits, some of which may indeed be virtues. Until we look at the causes, racists look like monsters who choose evil. There is nothing to say or examine except that they are awful, and no consideration of the deeper causes that must be changed to effectively combat racism. Racists are victimizers, and they cause terrible suffering; but when we refuse to consider the deeper causes and instead heap blame and moral responsibility on the racists, this is another case of blaming the victims.

10

BEYOND NEOLIBERALISM

At the core of neoliberalism is the supreme value of *property*. That is the heart of what Thomas Piketty calls the "proprietarian" ideology: the belief that the secure ownership of property is an absolute – or at least the most important and basic – right. The proprietarian ideology has powerful charms for many people, and Piketty describes them well:

> On the one hand, proprietarian ideology has an emancipatory dimension, which is real and should never be forgotten. On the other hand, it tends to bestow quasi-sacred status on existing property rights, regardless of origin or extent. This is just as real, and the inegalitarian and authoritarian consequences can be considerable.
>
> *(2020, 120)*

There are benefits to private property, but excessive and inequitable accumulation of property poses dangers. Private property enhances freedom, but concentration of property into a few hands encourages the authoritarian destruction of freedom.

Private property is not purely or even primarily the result of individual effort and decisions, but invariably depends on the community. As Piketty notes later in the same book:

> The question is not so much whether an item of property is a shared natural resource or a private good developed by a single individual, as all wealth is fundamentally social. Indeed, all wealth creation depends on the social division of labor and on the intellectual

DOI: 10.4324/9781003284680-10

> capital accumulated over the entire course of human history, which no living person can be said to own or claim as his or her personal achievement.
>
> *(2020, 562)*

While Piketty makes clear the social basis of property, the powerful American myth of "rugged individualism" often blinds people to that essential social support. Strengthened by frontier values, celebrated in cowboy westerns in which the individual hero fights for justice and then rides alone into the sunset ("Goodbye, Shane"), and personified by the straight talk and plain American values of John Wayne and Ronald Reagan, the basic right of the *individual* property holder is a powerful influence.

Closely connected with rugged individualism – the virtuous hard-working person needs no help from anyone – is the mantra of "I did it all myself," I owe nothing to anyone, and I am fully deserving of the just deserts of my accomplishments (in my case, the just deserts of prosperity; in your case, justly deserved poverty). Taking from me my justly deserved reward of wealth is wrong; providing it to alleviate the justly deserved poverty of the improvident compounds the injustice. Belief in just deserts and moral responsibility is the deep inner core of neoliberalism. The individual's accumulation of property and wealth (or lack thereof) is *justly deserved* because each individual has full moral responsibility for his or her choices and acts and efforts. Moral responsibility makes belief in a just world seem plausible. The suffering victim is not really an innocent victim (whether Augustine's sinful suffering infant, a rape victim, or an impoverished farmer) but in some obscure way must justly deserve to suffer; and prosperity and success – including enormously disproportionate wealth – are the justly deserved reward for virtue.

For neoliberals, the free market is the key to genuine freedom, and we deal freely in the market because we have the special powers of free choice and reason and will power required for free will. Each of us pursues our own *individual* free self-interested choices, we each accept full moral responsibility for the consequences of those choices, and "the invisible hand" of the free market produces the optimum economic outcome, the largest possible economic pie, with everyone receiving slices in accordance with their worth (and there is no standard of worth other than the judgment of the free market). When judged on its own merits, there is little plausibility in this mysterious and semi-divine account of the blessings of the free market. Viewed through the lens of a just world – everything, including the market, ultimately works out for the best – combined with a charming teleological tale of the invisible hand's wise and beneficent purposefulness, this nonsense often passes for wisdom.

Fairness

Challenging the entrenched neoliberal *system* – with its combination of free-market mysteries, property exaltation, radical individualism, and moral responsibility – is difficult; however, the problems generated by neoliberalism – gross economic inequity, massive pollution, mass imprisonment, elitism – are serious and obvious. Finding the most vulnerable point in the heavily defended neoliberal citadel is the first step in finding a path beyond the neoliberal system.

Fairness carries emotional punch. "That's not fair!" Most parents would swear that is the first three-word combination in early language acquisition. When a prep school student with all the advantages money can buy receives a special *legacy* bonus that gives the privileged student admission to an elite university in preference to a working-class student who built a better record while overcoming big obstacles, that is not *fair.* A low-paid parent works two full-time jobs in harsh conditions and stays precariously above the poverty line, one serious problem or illness from homelessness; while a man whose wealthy family smoothed his way to an Ivy League degree takes long tax-deductible alcohol-enhanced lunch breaks, often quits early, and "earns" eight times the combined wages of the parent working two full-time jobs, that's not *fair.* Joan has a supportive and nurturing childhood, and she develops strong powers of self-control, an eager inquisitiveness, a deeply confident level of cognitive self-efficacy, a resilient optimism, and a joyful cognitive profligacy. Jane's repressive and discouraging childhood saps her self-control and fortitude, minimizes her sense of cognitive self-efficacy, and shapes her as a pessimistic cognitive miser. Now as young adults, we say that their histories don't matter. Both are minimally competent so both are morally responsible for what they do or do not accomplish henceforward, and Joan justly deserves reward for her achievements while Jane is justly censured for her failures. That's not *fair.* The precise dimensions of fairness may be difficult to draw, but its importance and emotional force are undeniable.

Considerations of fairness challenge key elements of the neoliberal system. Moral responsibility and just deserts are at the core of the neoliberal system, and close consideration of fairness undermines them. Notwithstanding the American fascination with the "self-made man," it is clear that such exotic beings do not exist. For better or worse, we are all shaped by our long childhood dependency and early social and biological environments, as well as by our genetic legacies. Our successes and failures are ultimately the product of forces and influences we neither chose nor controlled. That is not to deny that people with great fortitude and resilience and creativity and cognitive ability can accomplish a great deal; but those vital factors that contributed to their success were not self-made, any more than lethargy and weak self-confidence and cognitive miserliness are self-made or self-chosen. It is not *fair* to hold people morally responsible for character traits and behavior that were ultimately beyond their control.

It is tempting to say that no matter how our characters developed, there is still a big difference between the industrious and the lethargic, and the hard work of the former should be rewarded while those who indulge in leisure and laziness also deserve the bitter fruits of their indolence (they have already enjoyed the *pleasures* of idleness). But indolence is not its own reward. It is more likely a symptom of depression or even extreme learned helplessness (Seligman 1975) and deep discouragement. Set aside the period of rest and restoration following hard labor, whether physical or cognitive. Focus on the periods when you were most industrious and diligent and compare them to times when you felt sapped of energy and uninspired and lethargic. Was the latter period more pleasant? Was such lethargy "its own reward"? And in any case, there is not a strong correlation between success and hard work. Whatever the American myth may say to the contrary, many of the hardest working people in our society are poor, and many of the wealthy are notoriously lazy.

Concern for *fairness* fuels the drive to make sense of moral responsibility. Large differences in wealth, comforts, *well-being* do not seem *fair*; but if we are *morally responsible* for those differences then they may be fair after all. If we somehow *made ourselves* that might provide grounds for our being morally responsible. But *causa sui* self-making is nonsense; and more modest models of self-making crash and burn on the problem of initial differences in self-making resources.

Markets and Fairness

Another element of the unified neoliberal system is the omniscient free market that makes "all things work together for good" for those who submit to the market and refrain from interfering in its free operations. Such a market may produce wealth, but it concentrates that wealth in a few hands. It also produces poverty and oligarchy, and much of the "wealth" is offset by damage to the environment. But the basic question is why anyone should suppose that an unregulated "free market" will function better than one that is judiciously regulated? And how could anyone suppose that the "free market" somehow maximizes human freedom? If not enmeshed in the neoliberal belief system, it is difficult to believe that a market dominated by concentrated wealth is just, or that it maximizes good for all, or that it enlarges our freedom. Wal-Mart used its massive power to drive small businesses and shopkeepers out. Unions were broken because manufacturers that were forced to play by Wal-Mart's rules could not afford to pay decent wages and either closed shop or moved to places where there were no union protections, while the Waltons became absurdly wealthy. At this point, you must sell through Amazon, and if Amazon wants to buy you out, they can "make you an offer you can't refuse." Is that an enhancement of freedom through the "free" market? The goal of many "start-ups" that receive massive venture capital funding is to "dominate a sector of the market" to such a degree that no serious competition can survive, and then exploit that control to generate profits – through monopolistic practices – that will more than offset large early losses. Such bully tactics are "not fair," but fairness has nothing to do with it. Perhaps in earlier centuries, when craftsmen and farmers brought their products to market and made useful exchanges, the free market was fair and mutually advantageous. The craftsman did not have the expertise and the land to produce crops effectively, and the farmer lacked the skills and the tools that made the craftsman's products better than those the farmer could have produced even with a much greater investment of time. But the marketplace of today is international, dominated by companies with gargantuan capital resources and huge advantages in knowledge and power. It is a marketplace in which accumulated wealth blocks entry for many people, and disparities of knowledge combined with psychologically sophisticated advertising destroy "informed" consumer preferences. Markets are valuable, as we have understood for millennia. They are not holy, nor omniscient, nor self-regulating, nor purposeful. The "invisible hand" of the free market is a farcical instance of teleological promiscuity run amok. Markets must be carefully regulated to prevent harm, abuse, and environmental disaster.

Free trade is too often a license to exploit. Consider the neoliberal principle that unless we are extracting the maximum economic benefit from "natural resources" they are being wasted and misused. That provides the justification for destroying wildlife preserves and national parks and vulnerable ecosystems. Western expansion "liberated" the land and its resources from indigenous peoples. They were not exploiting those "resources" effectively and enlightened proto-neoliberals had a right and an obligation to take the resources and use them productively. The same principle applies to the inefficient subsistence farming in Central America. US armed interference was not imperialism; it was instead the appropriation of land resources that were not being used efficiently and replacing small self-sustaining farms with large-scale plantation agriculture that maximized corporate profits. Stealing the land of small farmers was a neoliberal moral imperative.

Rejecting the Neoliberal System

The most obvious unfairness in the current neoliberal system is the grossly inequitable economy. According to Federal Reserve data, for the first quarter of 2021, the top 1% of Americans have a combined net worth of $41.5 trillion (32% of all household wealth in the United States). The top 10% have a combined net worth of $90 trillion (almost 70% of all household wealth). The bottom 50% of the population holds $2.6 trillion (2% of all wealth). In other words, the wealthiest 1% have almost 16 times the combined wealth of the bottom 50% of Americans. The trend for decades has been to concentrate wealth at the very top and leave almost nothing for those at the bottom: Federal Reserve data shows that since 1989 the wealth of the top 1% of US households has increased by eighteen percentage points while the total wealth controlled by the bottom 50% has been reduced by a third (Federal Reserve 2021). It seems to be a problem that will be difficult to fix, for two reasons. First, it appears that most Americans do not regard extreme differences in income and wealth as a serious problem (Davidai and Gilovich 2018, 297; Horowitz, Igielnik, and Kochhar 2020; Pew Research Center 2012). Second, there are powerful forces opposed to the needed changes, and those forces will fight to maintain their wealth and power. They have vast experience with systematic deception and exerting influence, including through "public service" advertising and "grass roots" (actually "astroturf") citizens groups. They have the economic power to punish those who oppose them (such as by shutting down factories and businesses and moving them to more complacent areas) and through punitive and expensive legal challenges. They have powerful political influence through lobbying and huge investments in political campaigns.

But the prospects for change are not as dark as they may appear. First, there are now many people who recognize the need for profound change. A recent Gallup poll (Younis 2019) found that while 51% of Americans believe socialism is bad, 43% favor some form of socialism. In 2016 and 2020, Bernie Sanders – an avowed socialist – had wide support in the Democratic primaries (especially among young voters) and was defeated only after the "moderate" power establishment in the Democratic Party united against his campaign. And while Americans may not regard inequitable distributions of wealth as the most pressing problem, they do recognize it as a problem: a 2020 Pew Research Center survey (Horowitz et al. 2020) found that 61% of Americans believe there is too much economic inequality in the country.

Second, Americans have deeply mistaken beliefs about the distribution of both income and wealth in the United States (Engelhardt and Wagener 2014; Hauser and Norton 2017; Niehues 2014; Norton and Ariely 2011), overestimating their own place in the wealth hierarchy and underestimating the systemic differences in wealth. In 1965, the average American CEO received 20 times the pay of the average employee of that company; in 2012, the ratio was 273 to 1 (Sabadish and Mishel 2013). Because CEO compensation can be difficult to calculate – much of the income comes from stock and stock options, which change in value; and should country club memberships and other special benefits count? – exact figures may vary, but The Economic Policy Institute placed the 2019 ratio at 320 to 1 (Mishel and Kandra 2020). In a 2014 study (Kiatpongsan and Norton 2014), American subjects estimated the ratio of CEO to worker pay as 29.6, roughly 10% of the actual number. The study also found wide agreement that the gap between workers and top management should be much smaller (approximately 6 to 1). The authors of the study concluded that there is broad consensus favoring much smaller pay gaps among workers at the top and the bottom and that the support for a smaller gap "holds in all subgroups of respondents regardless of the age, education, socioeconomic status, political affiliation, and opinions on inequality and pay" (Kiatpongsan and Norton 2014, 592). A national survey of Americans (Burak 2013) found that 61% favored placing a cap of 12 to 1 on the pay ratio of CEOs to their lowest-paid workers. When a 2011 study (Norton and Ariely 2011) of American subjects were offered an (unlabeled) choice between the wealth distribution in the United States (the top 20% of the population having 84% of the wealth, the next 20% having 11%, and the bottom 40% having less than ½ of 1%) and the much more even wealth distribution in Sweden (the top 20% hold 36% of the wealth) the Swedish distribution was preferred by 92% of American subjects. When subjects proposed their own ideal distributions, they were even more equal than the distribution in Sweden, with the wealthiest 20% receiving 32% of the wealth. As the authors of the study conclude:

> There was much more consensus than disagreement across groups from different sides of the political spectrum about this desire for a more equal distribution of wealth, suggesting that Americans may possess a commonly held "normative" standard for the distribution of wealth despite the many disagreements about policies that affect that distribution . . . .
>
> *Norton and Ariely 2011, 12*

Much of the supposed "complacency" regarding wealth and income distribution is based on ignorance of the real situation: a problem that can be solved, though not easily and not without opposition.

There is a third reason for optimism concerning American rejection of neoliberalism. A vital element of the "American Dream" is that America offers diligent workers abundant opportunities for social and economic advancement. Alesina, Stantcheva, and Teso (2018) cite John Steinbeck's whimsical but insightful assertion that Americans generally reject wealth redistribution because the working poor regard themselves as "temporarily embarrassed millionaires" (Steinbeck, *America and Americans*). That belief was probably strengthened by "frontier" opportunities in the 18th and 19th centuries and has remained part of the American myth ever since, even though America long ago ceased being "the land of opportunity" for economic mobility. As Thomas Piketty notes:

> No doubt the settler society of the early nineteenth century was more mobile. . . . Inherited wealth played a smaller role in the United States than in Europe, and US wealth was for a long time less concentrated, at least up to World War I. Throughout most of the twentieth century, however, and still today, the available data suggest that social mobility has been and remains lower in the United States than in Europe.
>
> *(2017, 617)*

Like the mistaken belief that income and wealth distribution is much more even than the actual extremes, belief in the possibility of upward mobility is one of the reasons for lack of opposition to the current economic distribution. In one study (Davidai and Gilovich 2015), participants estimated that a person born into the poorest 20% of the population had a 43% likelihood of rising to the top 60%; the actual chance is 30%. Contrary to cherished American myth, upward economic mobility is much less common in the United States than in most European countries.

> In countries like Finland, Norway, and Denmark, the tie between parental economic status and the adult earnings of children is weakest: less than one-fifth of any economic advantage or disadvantage that a father may have had in his time is passed on to a son in adulthood. In Italy, the United Kingdom, and the United States, roughly 50 percent of any advantage or disadvantage is passed on
>
> *(Corak 2016, 81)*

A study by Alesina, Stantcheva, and Teso (2018) found that "Americans vastly overestimate the probability of making it to the top of the ladder for children starting from the bottom" (2018, 532); similar results – "across four studies, . . . participants . . . exhibited substantial and consistent overestimates of class mobility" – were found by Kraus and Tan (2015, 110). Studies by Davidai and Gilovich found that when asked about US ranking in social mobility among a list of 15 countries (among which the US ranked 8th) 75% of the subjects placed the United States in the top 3, and more than half believed that the US has the greatest mobility of any of the countries; and in another study rating the United States among the G7 countries (where the US ranks 5th in mobility), 75% of the subjects placed the United States in the top 3, and 55% believed that the United States ranked first (Davidai and Gilovich 2018, 301). As noted by the OECD, "Intergenerational earnings mobility is low in countries with high inequality such as Italy, the United Kingdom, and the United States, and much higher in the Nordic countries, where income is distributed more evenly" (2011, 40). While the reality is otherwise, the American myth of rich opportunities for upward mobility is deeply rooted: "Even if Americans are not more socially mobile than Europeans, most American family histories include an episode where some first American left a poorer European country (especially Ireland, Italy, and Eastern Europe) for much richer America. This experience was real and one might think that it must play some role in the beliefs about the bounty of the American economy" (Alesina and Glaeser 2004, 190).

The "American dream" is a key selling point of the neoliberal system, from the proto-neoliberal late 18th century through the contemporary neoliberal era of 1980 to the present. Because Americans (at least those who are not enslaved) live in a "land of freedom" and have remarkable powers of self-making free will, everyone has the opportunity to succeed financially, no matter their background or starting point. The Horatio Alger "rags to riches" stories (or at least rags to solid middle-class comfort) promoted the belief that even the poorest young boy could – through honesty and effort – rise to financial success.

Research by Kraus and Tan demonstrates that although the America myth of upward mobility has long since lost any plausibility it may have had, it is still fervently believed:

> The United States is faced with record levels of income inequality and one of the lowest rates of social mobility among industrial nations (Burkhauser, Feng, Jenkins, & Larrimore, 2012; Fiske and Markus 2012; Piketty and Saez 2001). Despite these constraints on economic opportunities, Americans place significant hope on the American Dream – the promise that individuals, from any sector of society, have an equal opportunity to become better educated, earn more money, and obtain whatever job they desire. These beliefs in social class mobility are widespread.
>
> *Kraus and Tan 2015, 101*

The results of their four studies confirm how deep, pervasive, and substantial this false belief in American mobility remains:

> American culture is filled with anecdotes about the promise of equal opportunity and the pursuit of happiness. Beliefs in the American Dream permeate our parenting decisions, educational practices, and political agendas, and yet . . . Americans are largely inaccurate when asked to describe actual trends in social class mobility in society. Across four studies, samples of online survey participants and university students exhibited substantial and consistent overestimates of class mobility – overestimating the amount of income mobility and educational access in society by a wide margin
>
> *Kraus and Tan 2015, 109–110*

When Americans learn that the "upward mobility," American Dream has been badly broken by contemporary neoliberalism, "complacency" concerning an unjust economic system (and its inequitable distribution of resources) may be transformed into deep opposition. Studies by McCall, Burk, Laperriere, and Richeson suggest that increasing levels of economic inequality reduce belief in upward mobility: "The results of the present study offer compelling support for the hypothesis that one outcome of exposure to information about rising economic inequality is the increased perception that the opportunity structure of American society may be less open than previously assumed"

(2017, 3). In an additional larger study, the researchers found that reduced belief in economic opportunity significantly increased the belief that both business and government have a responsibility to address the problem of economic inequality (2017, 5). As they summarize their research findings, "The present work offered clear and consistent evidence regarding the causal relationship between exposure to information about rising inequality and beliefs about opportunity – beliefs that may subsequently shape support for equity-enhancing policies" (2017, 5). Increasing economic inequality reduces confidence in opportunities for upward mobility, and that drop in confidence encourages positive consideration of programs that will reduce the inequality. The great defense of economic inequity is that it is based on meritocracy, and that claim requires genuine opportunity for upward mobility through the combination of talent and hard work, the disproportionate share of wealth held by those at the top of the economic scale is justified because of their hard work and their own merits. If such opportunities are not available then the justification for large-scale inequality in wealth and income collapses, and the fundamental unfairness of the neoliberal system becomes clear.

Conclusion

The United States is deeply divided, but there are still enduring points of agreement and some deep common values – such as fairness and opportunity – on which to build. Americans may be uncomfortably aware that American practice has not lived up to American values, but they believe that the United States has come much closer to achieving those goods than it actually has: that America is still the land of opportunity and a land where wealth and income are distributed in something that resembles fairness. Those beliefs are mistaken, opportunities for social mobility in America are well below those in Europe, and the distribution of wealth is not only far more inequitable than most people believe but even further from what most people regard as fair. The essential task is making that knowledge widely available. The belief that the United States *should* be the land of opportunity is a central part of the American dream, and that is a wonderful ideal. It is not an ideal that America has ever lived up to – certainly not during the shameful era of slavery or the disgraceful era of Jim Crow violence, and not now as the United States falls behind Europe in opportunities for successful upward mobility. Recognizing that we are currently moving further from achieving that ideal does not mean that we should abandon it, but that we should study how our pursuit of that ideal has gone wrong and what we can do to move toward achievement of that worthy goal. The first step toward fixing what is wrong is *recognizing* what is wrong.

When people become aware that the distribution of property is fundamentally unfair – that it is not based on working harder or contributing more, and it is not based on legitimate competition with fair opportunity for success and upward mobility – then the special reverence for private property is challenged. When people have been enslaved and their labor stolen from them by violent coercive measures, then the private property that the slave "owners" accumulated is not their rightful property. When the economic system privileges some and handicaps others, the resulting distribution of private property has no special protected status. Private property remains important, but distribution of private property should be much fairer, as a large majority of Americans agree when informed of the distortions of the present system. That is precisely what the elitist framers of the Constitution feared: an informed public that would demand their fair share of the wealth and genuine control of their government. Americans do not favor strict equality; indeed, few people think that could work. We need economic incentives, and capital accumulation is essential for launching important projects. But we do not need the grossly unfair neoliberal system.

The key to rejecting the neoliberal system is broader recognition of the nature of that system and its effects. More people must understand how resources are being distributed under that system: the extreme disparity between the wealth at the top, the struggle for the middle class, and the economic desperation of millions of people at the lower end. There must be broader knowledge of the increasing rigidity of the economic classes, reduced opportunities for advancement, and the enormous harm and profound peril of environmental degradation. People from all walks of life can contribute their lived experience to a richer understanding: factory workers, firefighters, lawyers, postal workers, farmers, professors, food workers, nurses, truck drivers, programmers, secretaries, construction workers. All of us have much to learn about how neoliberal economic policies have ravaged society and ruined lives and destroyed hopes, and all of us have something to teach.

11

REPLACING NEOLIBERALISM

The center of the American neoliberal system – and the source of its power – is the enormous concentration of wealth controlled by a tiny percentage of the population. It not only impoverishes many for the luxuries of a few but also gives disproportionate political power to a small group of very wealthy people. There is nothing wrong with private property, markets, and capital accumulation; to the contrary, all of these are valuable elements of a well-functioning economic system. But for the system to work efficiently, the capital must circulate rather than being concentrated long-term in a few hands. That circulation empowers people with fresh ideas and provides opportunities that will not be choked off by those with massive capital and the power to buy out or destroy competition.

Effective redistribution of the massive wealth held by the top 1% (and especially the top .1%) cannot be accomplished with a slightly more – or even a substantially more – progressive income tax (not even if the tax dodges and tax shelters could be closed). A more progressive income tax is important, but serious changes to the concentration of wealth will require other forms of taxation. As Thomas Piketty writes:

> Progressive taxes on inheritances and income must again play the role that they used to play in the twentieth century when rates in the United States and United Kingdom ran as high as 70-90 percent on the highest incomes and largest fortunes for decades – decades in which growth rose to unprecedented levels. . . . They need to be complemented by a progressive annual tax on wealth, which I see as the central tool for achieving true circulation of capital. . . . The wealth tax is more difficult to manipulate than the income tax, particularly for the very

DOI: 10.4324/9781003284680-11

> wealthy, whose taxable income is often a small fraction of their wealth, while their actual economic income accumulates in family holdings or special-purpose vehicles.
>
> *(2020, 976)*

Estate taxes (inheritance taxes) are unpopular in the United States. No doubt much of that unpopularity is based on misinformation spread by the very wealthy: false stories of small farmers losing the family farm because of ruinous estate taxes, when in fact estate taxes are imposed only on huge fortunes – and even those taxes are largely avoided with the help of clever tax lawyers. But whatever the cause, the unpopularity – together with the inefficiency – of estate taxes provides good reason to minimize their use. On the other hand, wealth taxes – similar to property taxes, but on much larger fortunes – are regarded as more acceptable, even popular. A Hill-HarrisX survey (conducted Feb. 1–2, 2019) found that 74% of registered voters back an annual 2% tax on people with assets over $50 million, and a 3% tax on people with assets in excess of $1 billion (for those with assets valued at $51 million, the tax would be $20,000 – they will not be forced to sell their ski lodges at Aspen). Sixty-five percent of Republican voters supported it, along with 69% of Independents and 86% of Democratic voters. It had the support of 73% of Western and Midwestern voters, 72% of Southern voters, and 78% of Northeastern voters (Hill-HarrisX, The 2019). If the United States were democratic rather than oligarchic such a wealth tax would pass easily; the fact that passing such legislation would be a steep uphill battle shows the true status of "American democracy."

Empowering Workers, Empowering Citizens

A more progressive tax system – including an annual wealth tax – is an essential and popular element of any effort to move from neoliberalism to a more democratic and equitable society, but it is only one part of the effort to reach that goal. There must be opportunities for more people to exercise real control in their work and their communities and their country, and that requires positive changes in the way businesses and workplaces operate. One of the most promising – and already proven – models for achieving that goal is through *co-management* of corporations. As Piketty notes, implementing co-management "has helped the Germanic and Nordic countries to develop an economic and social model that is more productive and less inegalitarian" (2020, 973).

In co-management, workers have voting rights within the companies in which they work, typically by having workers' representatives as voting members of boards of directors. In Germany, half of the boards are made up of workers' representatives; in Sweden, approximately one-third. Co-management places people on the board who care about the long-term success of the company, rather than the profits or stock price for the next year or two. Those board members live in the community rather than flying in on private jets for a board meeting. They have an interest in what the company contributes to the community and in promoting and preserving the well-being of the community and the environment and the workers. And they will not approve grossly inflated salaries for the CEO and other corporate officers.

Today corporate officers serve on several corporate boards: interlocking boards where all the board members (CEOs or CFOs at various companies) take care of one another more than the company. Bill from Company A votes an enormous salary for Joe from Company B, who approves a huge salary for Frank, the CEO of company C, and Frank in turn happily endorses an absurd salary for Bill. In exchange for this reciprocal back-scratching, everyone gets a nice bonus for "serving" on several corporate boards. Piketty (2017) notes that since 1980, the level of income inequality in the United States has soared: for 30 years, from 1950 to 1980, the top 10% received 33–35% of all income; since 1980, the income of the top 10% has rapidly increased to near 50% of total income:

> This spectacular increase in inequality largely reflects an unprecedented explosion of very elevated incomes from labor, a veritable separation of the top managers of large firms from the rest of the population. One possible explanation of this is that the skills and productivity of these top managers rose suddenly in relation to those of other workers. Another explanation, which to me seems more plausible and turns out to be much more consistent with the evidence, is that those top managers by and large have the power to set their own remuneration, in some cases without limit and in many cases without any clear relation to their individual productivity.
>
> *Piketty 2017, 32–33*

The worker board members are likely to have a clearer sense of the real worth of the corporate officers and no incentive to approve excessive salaries. They also have a genuine concern for the workers, as well as realizing that the company must survive for everyone's benefit: not for a year or two, but long-term to fund pensions. The CEO can bankrupt the company, ride out on a golden parachute, and – with the help of wealthy friends and co-conspirators – land another job as a CEO while the workers at the former company face loss of their jobs and their pensions. Board members who are also workers will not have such a comfortable landing if the company fails.

Systems and Commitment

Co-management is not the only way that workers can make a valuable contribution to workplace decision-making. Another – already successfully used in some US industries (as well as in several medical facilities) – is the *systems* approach (Shimbun 1988; Shingo 1986). Originating in Japan, the systems approach transformed the manufacturing process at Toyota. From producing cars that had become a symbol of shoddy workmanship, Toyota became a leader in the manufacture of cars valued for their reliability and absence of manufacturing flaws. *Jidoka* is a vital part of the systems model at Toyota:

> *Jidoka* is one of the core principles of the Toyota Production System. It means applying the "human touch" to immediately address manufacturing problems at the moment they are detected. *Jidoka* is used at Toyota to empower every worker to stop the assembly line whenever a quality problem is detected. The worker pulls a red cord and the entire assembly line stops, idling every machine and every worker on that line until the problem is solved or a remedy is found to prevent a defect from moving forward. When the line stops, fellow workers run over to the person who pulled the red cord to help them resolve the problem.
>
> *Bodek 2011*

Jidoka involves an intense effort to detect problems as early as possible, including emphasis on discovering and announcing *potential* problems; and an insistence that the source of the problem must be discovered and fixed at its *roots*: the flaw lurking deep in the system must be found and corrected. If a line worker makes a mistake, the deep problem is *not* solved by blaming and reprimanding or replacing the worker. Instead, the query must ask what in the system caused the worker's mistake? Was the worker inadequately trained? Was the worker placed in a position unsuitable for the worker's abilities? Is there something in the production line (bad labels, bad procedures, confusing steps, poor design, failed safeguards) that makes such an error likely?

The traditional process of blaming and shaming the worker has two great flaws: first, the assumption that the individual worker is the problem (the problem is solved when the worker is blamed or replaced) blocks the deeper inquiry that exposes core systemic problems; second, when workers are "blamed and shamed" they cover up errors as much as possible, product quality suffers, and small covered-up problems evolve into larger problems. In the *jidoka* process, one who reports errors – including one's own – is esteemed as someone who is working to make the system better.

In addition to focusing on systems and rejection of blame and shame, there is another important element of *jidoka*: respect for the intelligence and ability and contributions of *all* workers, rather than a top-down model in which managers have a monopoly on intelligence and insight and workers are passive cogs in the machine. Workers have a vital role in understanding how the system is supposed to work and detecting – and fixing – the problems when it doesn't. All workers use their intelligence and vigilance to detect problems and find ways to solve them, all workers are empowered to halt production when there is a problem, and the expertise and intelligence of every worker is respected and valued.

The success of the systems approach led to its adoption in other industries and other settings, including in air traffic control. Air traffic control was plagued by problems, including catastrophic errors and a workforce suffering from sleep-disorders, depression, drug and alcohol abuse, and other stress-related problems. Controllers worked in a complex and demanding system with constant handoffs from and to different regions, flight names and instructions that were often similar, few internal controls to catch errors, and a culture that treated all errors as the result of individual negligence: errors that could easily result in disasters. Controllers hid errors whenever possible or tried to shift the blame, and the hidden errors were repeated until they became terrifying near misses that were "solved" by firing the "negligent" controllers. The not surprising result was airline catastrophes.

When air traffic control switched to a systems model – which sought systemic causes for errors rather than blaming hard-working controllers doing a difficult job – the atmosphere changed dramatically (Harris and Muir 2005). Instead of hiding errors or blaming others, controllers reported all errors (including "harmless" errors that were previously hidden) and were commended for finding flaws in the system. Rather than constantly suspecting others of making them scapegoats, everyone worked together to collect information on the systemic sources of errors to fix problems before they caused harm – and to build a system that would provide safeguards against errors and quickly detect and fix the inevitable errors (Sabatini 2008).

Sometimes controllers were causing problems and making mistakes; but if so, that was also valuable systemic information: what was causing once competent controllers to burnout? What was the gap in the way controllers were selected or trained? A controller might be retrained or reassigned, but not blamed and punished, shamed, and fired. Finding a flawed controller was the start of a deeper inquiry into systemic problems, not the end of an inquiry culminating in individual blame and dismissal. Alexandru Grama, a Romanian air traffic controller, summed up the benefits of the systems approach for aviation safety:

> Sometimes it seems that organisations expect perfection from their imperfect employees; imperfect performance is considered unacceptable. This way, individuals are reluctant to come forward with their mistakes. They only become obvious to everyone when serious incidents or accidents occur, but then it is already too late. Punishing imperfect performance does not make the organisation safer. Instead it makes the remaining individuals less willing to improve the system. Just culture [a version of the systems approach] enables the transition from 'punishing imperfect individuals' to a 'self improving system'. It supports better outcomes over time using the same resources, based on the trust and

> willingness of individuals to report issues. . . . It is a continuous process that allows an organisation to become safer every day by listening to employees.
>
> *quoted in Shorrock et al. 2014, 13*

Hospitals are another place where errors can and do have terrible results. Patient safety experts calculated that over an eight-year period, approximately 250,000 deaths each year were caused by medical error (Makary and Daniel 2016). Most of those fatal errors occurred in hospitals. Hospital care is a complex and often stressful process, and opportunities for errors are rife. To reduce the errors, many hospitals have adopted the systems approach – sometimes with great success, but also with strong resistance. The basic problems in hospital care mirror the larger problems in neoliberal culture. Elitism and devotion to individual moral responsibility block deeper inquiry, undermine cooperative efforts to prevent errors, and focus blame on those lower in the hierarchy. Lucian Leape describes the fundamental problem:

> Physicians are socialized in medical school and residency to strive for error-free practice. There is a powerful emphasis on perfection, both in diagnosis and treatment. In everyday hospital practice, the message is equally clear: mistakes are unacceptable. Physicians are expected to function without error, an expectation that physicians translated into the need to be infallible. One result is that physicians, not unlike test pilots, come to view an error as a failure of character – you weren't careful enough, you didn't try hard enough. This kind of thinking lies behind a common reaction by physicians: "How can there be an error without negligence?"
>
> . . . this need to be infallible creates a strong pressure to intellectual dishonesty, to cover up mistakes rather than to admit them. The organization of medical practice, particularly in the hospital, perpetuates these norms. Errors are rarely admitted or discussed among physicians in private practice. Physicians typically feel, not without reason, that admission of error will lead to censure or increased surveillance or, worse, that their colleagues will regard them as incompetent or careless. Far better to conceal a mistake or, if that is impossible, to try to shift the blame to another, even the patient.
>
> *Leape 1994, 1851–1852*

Mistakes by air traffic controllers were often impossible to hide, but in medicine, the entire medical profession unites to hide mistakes, and even medical errors that result in tragic deaths are often concealed. An anesthesiologist administers an adult-sized dose to an infant, resulting in severe brain damage and ultimately death. What went wrong? The infant was undergoing surgery, and so there were already significant problems, a weakened heart gave out, an organ shut down. There are many possible "explanations," and if the medical community bands together to protect the errant anesthesiologist – who after all is one of us, and a good friend, and we must close ranks to defend against those predatory malpractice lawyers – then the error may never be revealed, and its deeper cause never discovered or examined or fixed. Under the systems approach, the focus is on *fixing* a failure of the larger *system*. When there is a mistake, we all shared the mistake, a mistake we profoundly regret, and – as promoted by "Sorry Works" (Wojcieszak, Banja, and Houk 2006; Simons 2007) – if there was harm, then we sincerely apologize to the victim or the victim's family, strive to correct the damage to the degree possible, and work together to find the root cause and make the system better and safer.

The Opposition

The deep opposition to the Systems "beyond blame and shame" approach displays the problems – rooted in radical individualism and moral responsibility – at the heart of both bad medical practice and neoliberalism. Edmund Pellegrino is the most trenchant philosophical critic of employing the systems approach in medicine, and his criticisms are important in understanding the fierce opposition. The basic problem is evident in the "solution" to medical error proposed by Pellegrino:

> Preventable or negligent harm as the result of error is a moral failure, whatever its legal status may be. Moral blame and culpability are therefore unavoidable. . . . There are. . . dangers of complacency and dulling of the moral sensibilities of the humans in the system when either a "blame-free" approach or a "blame-the-system" approach is adopted. The power of individual guilt can be constructive as often as it is destructive. Personal accountability is owed to the person injured. The deterrent effect of fear of shame and blame is not safely ignored.
>
> *(2004, 86)*

It is true that the deterrent effect of blame and shame is not safely ignored, but the major deterrent effect is deterring the reporting and examining and understanding of errors and their sources. And the "complacency and dulling" that Pellegrino fears are enhanced by the cover-ups that the blame system promotes. I can be complacent, because there wasn't a mistake at all (since no one could find it) or because the problem was *really* caused by someone else (usually a nurse, but sometimes the patient) to whom the blame was shifted. Diligent effort to find and fix the real problems – problems that are often deep and difficult – is the opposite of complacency.

Pellegrino offers a "personal integrity" and "individual character" solution to the problem of medical error – try harder, concentrate constantly, be virtuous, honor the ideals of your profession. His "solution" focuses attention on the specific individual who is at most the end actor in a complex causal series and ignores the systemic problems causing error, burnout, and negligence. But Pellegrino insists that the only legitimate path to better health care must be through focus on *individuals* who bear complete responsibility – and deserve full blame or credit – for both medical success and medical error:

> The blame-free approach advocated by many in the patient-safety movement cannot erase the individual moral onus of preventable error. The physician or other health professional cannot blame the system for his or her failings. Organizational conformity cannot take the place of moral responsibility even if the system follows a no-blame rule. The physician or the nurse, in their respective realms, are the pathways through which harm or good comes to the patient. They are responsible for what they order, or the way they follow an order or procedure. They are responsible for monitoring the steps immediately preceding and following their personal functions in that process.
>
> *(2004, 88)*

Physicians and nurses often "are the pathways through which harm or good comes to the patient," but they function in complex systems, and improving those systems requires open deep scrutiny of the systems by all involved, without fear or favor. Blaming not only prevents the openness that is the pathway such investigations must follow, but it also calls a sharp halt to the inquiry by its insistence that the buck stops with this *individual* who justly deserves blame. The problem may be in overwork or too much pressure, or "accidents waiting to happen" (such as medications that look almost identical or the names of which are easily confusing). When something goes wrong, it is better to look hard for the systemic problem, rather than narrowly focusing attention and blame on the last person in the causal chain.

The systems approach not only rejects blame and shame but also rejects rigid hierarchy. *Everyone* is part of the effort to discover small errors that might become catastrophes, everyone contributes intelligence and experience and alertness to catch potential errors before they happen, and everyone participates in the effort to improve the system so that errors are reduced. Physician Bruce Davis cherishes the *opposite* approach: physicians – and especially surgeons – are at the top of the hierarchy, and those who are not among the elite cannot understand and have nothing to offer:

> The key here is that it is PEER review – review by other surgeons engaged in the same type of practice. I don't recognize a committee

> made up of an Internist, a Pathologist, a Cardiologist, and an Orthopedic Surgeon as a committee of my peers. They don't do what I do. They don't face the same decisions and problems that I do and have no frame of reference from which to analyze my actions.
>
> *Davis 2015*

This scornful attitude toward anyone not in my elite group is manifested in a remark concerning Lucian Leape, one of the leaders in the systems approach to reducing medical error. Davis describes "Dr. Lucian Leape, a professor of PUBLIC HEALTH (emphasis mine);" and he concludes that Dr. Leape cannot help because "He is also not a surgeon. He does not understand the culture of the M & M conference and its power to offer both correction and forgiveness." The scornful dismissal of Leape as a professor of public health who is "not a surgeon" also reveals the attitude toward others on the surgical team: "She's a NURSE," and so has nothing to offer in preventing errors and improving processes; her only job is to be quiet, follow my orders without question, and be deferential. In this atmosphere, no one dares to raise concerns and prevent mistakes, and the only person in the room allowed to raise questions is too arrogant to admit there is a problem.

The no-blame systems model reduces errors, increases cooperation, and treats all workers with respect. In the process, it has a leveling effect on hierarchy. It is not only physicians and managers who are important, but everyone plays an important role in detecting and avoiding errors and improving the system, and everyone brings dedication and intelligence, and perceptiveness to making the system work better. Nurses and technicians are essential players in watching for mistakes and making improvements in processes and preventing errors: when they see a potential problem, they call a halt and everyone on the team works *together* to avoid the danger, and the problem – or potential problem – is carefully reported so that systemic solutions can be found. For those who believe in the importance of *everyone* exercising intelligent control, and the importance of everyone having a commitment to improving the organization through cooperative efforts and intelligence and dedication, this changed perspective is a substantial benefit. Reducing errors works best by increasing opportunities for workers to exercise control and strengthen their self-confidence and enhance their dedication to the positive goals of the organization.

Commitment vs. Control

The systems model meshes smoothly and productively with the *commitment* model of management. The commitment model is profoundly different from the top-down management style of the traditional *control* model. In the control model, the goal is for workers to passively obey orders without question.

Orders are enforced and workers are motivated through threat of punishment, and they must submit to the wisdom of their superiors:

> The control-based model assumes that people are incapable of self-regulating their behaviors, and they need constant guidance, reward, and discipline from management. Consistent with this assumption, the natural emphasis of the control-based management is on monitoring employee behavior closely via a variety of control mechanisms. . . . In a control-based organization, hierarchy is tall and communication is quite anemic, mostly top-down. The focus of employee behaviors is on compliance, with procedures, instructions, and orders from the top.
>
> *Khatri, Brown, and Hicks 2009, 316*

The control model of management seems natural in a neoliberal culture in which rational freedom is exclusively for the elite, while the masses – who lack powers of self-control – must be closely monitored, effectively controlled, and compelled to submit to the judgment of the market and of their betters.

When workers are treated as objects to be monitored and controlled the result is a punitive system that sinks into a destructive cycle:

> The ubiquity of control-based management in health care organizations seems to be a major source of the culture of blame existing in them. . . . The control-based management does not allow much learning to take place in the health care delivery process and sets in motion a "vicious cycle" in which greater incidence of medical errors leads to greater control and regulation of employee behaviors, further strengthening the blame culture and finger pointing.
>
> *Khatri et al. 2009, 316*

Control-based top-down management assumes that productive work requires close monitoring, strict rules, and harsh discipline. When a problem occurs, the *individual* who caused the problem is punished and the problem is solved, no deeper inquiry is required. Management makes the plans and controls the operations, and workers follow management directives with as little variation as possible. Improving the process is the job of management, not workers.

In contrast to control-based management, commitment-based management encourages worker autonomy and participation in decision-making and intelligent efforts to improve the process and the product, and every worker makes a valuable contribution to the success of the shared enterprise:

> The commitment-based management, on the other hand, has two underlying assumptions: (a) People are capable of self-discipline, and given the opportunity and developmental experiences, they would like to seek

> responsibility and exercise initiative, and (b) people work best when they are fully committed to the organization, and they commit to the organization when they are trusted and allowed to work autonomously. The commitment-based approach relies on creating an environment that encourages the exercise of initiative, ingenuity, and self-direction on the part of employees in achieving organizational goals.
>
> *Khatri et al. 2009, 316*

The intelligence and commitment and expertise of workers are respected, management and workers share a common goal, and workers enjoy substantial autonomy and control in producing work they value.

Like the systems model, the commitment model is good for business. The increased decision-making and autonomy of workers in the systems-commitment model is also good for democracy. It is absurd to expect workers to spend their working lives under closely controlled conditions that reward passivity and then magically transform into careful critical thinkers and active participants when engaged in the political process.

Free Will

Emphasis on blame and shame discourages deeper inquiry and promotes an elitist division between management and workers. Moral responsibility blocks better understanding, promotes harsh punitive measures and the inequitable distribution of wealth, props up belief in a just world (which in turn encourages blaming the victim), joins forces with radical individualism, and forms the dark heart of neoliberalism. Additional harm arises from desperate efforts to find *grounds* for moral responsibility because free will seems the most promising foundation for moral responsibility, the obsessive effort to make free will support moral responsibility has twisted free will into remarkably implausible forms. When free will is liberated from the impossible burden of moral responsibility and rescued from the clutches of neoliberalism, then a more plausible and beneficial account of free will emerges.

If evolution rather than creationism is correct, then free will is not a special divine gift given to humans made in the image of God, but instead something that evolved because of its survival value; and it can be found in various forms in many other species (Waller 2015). When free will is not the unique human grounds for moral responsibility, then we can study free will from a larger evolutionary perspective in a wide variety of foraging animals (animals that, like humans, are neither super rational nor *causa sui* deities).

Like many fortunate discoveries, one vitally important element of free will was elucidated when the researcher was seeking something else entirely. J. Lee Kavanau was studying learning processes in feral white-footed mice but was frustrated by the fact that having mastered the maze the mice continued to make mistakes, taking an occasional wrong turn away from the food reward. This frustration led Kavanau to an important insight into animal free will:

> Actually, these responses are incorrect only from the point of view of the investigator's rigidly prescribed program, not from that of the animal. The basis for these responses is that the animal has a certain degree of variability built into many of its behavior patterns. This variability is adaptive to conditions in the wild, where there are many relationships that are not strictly prescribed. . . . The habit of deviating fairly frequently from stereotyped "correct" responses, together with a high level of spontaneous activity, underlie the remarkable facility with which white-footed mice can be taught to cope with complex contingencies.
>
> *(1967, 1628)*

Choices are important, and the choices we need – whether humans, baboons, or white-footed mice – are neither mysterious nor miraculous. In most circumstances, choice is inherently appealing, and like many other animals, humans favor choices for their own sake (Bown, Read, and Summers 2003; Morris and Royle 1988). This strong preference for choices makes sound evolutionary sense: "Given that food supplies sometimes may be lost to competitors or may disappear in other ways, an organism that chooses patches of the environment in which two or more food supplies are available will probably have a survival advantage over one that chooses patches of the environment containing only a single food supply" (Catania and Sagvolden 1980, 85).

Later researchers affirmed the importance of having choices:

> We suggest that a preference for choice over no-choice is a heuristic that has emerged because, in evolutionary terms, it has usually led to the best outcome. Our ancestors would have quickly learned that it is better to hunt in an area where there is a choice of prey (both in number and species), than in an area where there is little if any choice. Indeed, it is likely that they would not have had to learn at all – the research showing that animals prefer choice over no-choice paths . . . suggests that the preference for choice may be a fundamental part of our natural endowment.
>
> *Bown et al. 2003, 307*

The depth of the need and desire for choice is indicated by a study of the neural substrates that respond to the anticipated opportunity for making a choice. Leotti and Delgado "tested whether the mere anticipation of personal involvement through choice would recruit reward related brain circuitry, particularly the striatum" (2011, 1311), and they found:

> behavioral evidence that choice is desirable, and, furthermore, we found that anticipating an opportunity for choice was associated with increased

> activity in a network of brain regions thought to be involved in reward processing. Collectively, the findings suggest that simply having the opportunity to choose is inherently valuable in some situations.
>
> These results provide empirical evidence supporting the hypothesis that the need for control – and the need for choice – is biologically motivated.
>
> *Leotti and Delgado 2011, 1314; see also Bjork and Hommer 2007*

Whether a mouse in a maze or a shopper in a supermarket, we value choice-making. But moral responsibility distorts choice-making into something that has no value for mice or men. The super choices that are supposed to support moral responsibility are made independently of any influences or control or values, choices made in a vacuum, with *nothing* determining the outcome – nothing *causing* the first cause choice – except the special choice itself. But we do not need choices that transcend all interests and environmental influences; rather, we need choices generated by and adapted to our environments and needs and desires.

Some promote a view of free will that denies the importance of choice and instead equates free will with effective *control*. But just as the first group distorted choice (in an effort to make it support moral responsibility) so the second group exaggerates the nature of control; and to make matters worse, they treat control as a *competitor* to choice, insisting that open choices are not *required* for free will (Harry Frankfurt 1971; John Martin Fischer 2007, 82) or even claiming (Wolf 1990) that open choices are an *impediment* to genuine free will.

Susan Wolf insists that the only *real* freedom is following the *right* path for the right reasons: free will requires following the straight and narrow path that tracks the True and Good. This view has a long history. For Aristotle, true freedom consists in following the narrow path of godlike *reason*. For Christianity, true freedom requires perfect obedience to God. For Wolf, genuine freedom requires accurately tracking the path of an objective True and Good, without deviations: ". . . we can state the condition of freedom and responsibility more directly by referring outright to the ability to act in accordance with (and on the basis of) the True and the Good" (1990, 73). Seeking alternatives means straying from the one true path of genuine freedom.

The capacity to stray from the narrow rational path would be an ability to act *ir*rationally, and for Wolf that "is a very strange ability to want, if it is any ability at all" (1990, 56). Wolf's account of free will is a good fit for the right environment: the perfect, eternal, and unchanging environment of the cherubims and seraphims and other Heavenly hosts; and also, for the neoliberal world, where the only "freedom" is humble submission to the True and Good free market. But for foraging animals in a changing environment that must be explored and controlled, the straight and narrow path has fatal disadvantages. When we try new paths and new ideas – when we make choices – we make "mistakes" that deviate from the fixed known narrow path but are often beneficial, leading to valuable discoveries. The attraction to choices and exploration and trying new and sometimes mistaken paths is a vital element of healthy animal free will. Rather than an enemy of effective control, it is an essential partner.

Philosophical accounts of free will typically endorse and exaggerate either choice (distorting it into *causa sui* first cause choice) or control (making it a narrow purely rational process of absolute control), and then treat the other element of free will as of little or no importance or even (as in Wolf's case) worse than useless. But viewed from a broader biological perspective – considering the free will that evolved in foraging animals such as humans – *both* choice and control are essential, and rather than competitors they are vital complementary elements of free will that must function in close harmony. Björn Brembs makes the relationship clear:

> Beyond behaving unpredictably to evade predators or outcompete a competitor, all animals must explore, must try out different solutions to unforeseen problems. Without behaving variably, without acting rather than passively responding, there can be no success in evolution. Those individuals who have found the best balance between flexible actions and efficient responses are the ones who have succeeded in evolution. It is this potential to behave variably, to initiate actions independently of the stimulus situation, which provides animals with choices.
>
> *Brembs 2010*

Bremb's "flexible actions" are choices, and his "efficient responses" are control. Animals that cannot effectively exert control to exploit a beneficial source have little chance of survival, but animals that focus too narrowly on a currently productive source and neglect exploration of alternatives are imperiled when the current source is exhausted. Dan Dennett – a philosopher with a rich appreciation of psychological and biological research – clearly recognizes the importance of *both* control and choice for a free will that is psychologically healthy:

> We all always want . . . lots of elbow room. We want a margin for error, we want to keep our options open, so that our chances of maintaining control over our operations, come what may, are enhanced.
>
> *(1984, 63)*

And in addition to the elbow room of open options:

> We very definitely do not want to lose control or be out of control or be controlled by something or someone else – like a marionette or puppet. We want to be *in control*, and to control both ourselves and our destinies.
>
> *(1984, 51)*

Control and choice are the key elements of free will (Waller 2011; Waller 2015), and human animals do not flourish in circumstances that diminish their powers and opportunities for choice and control – whether the circumstances are the home, the school, the assembly line, the political sphere, or a long-term care facility. We want to work in environments that fulfill those needs, not controlled like puppets. Finding better ways to do things, exploring options, and exercising control improve productivity and promotes psychological well-being. In contrast, blame and shame make us fearful of exploring better paths and finding better means of control. Neoliberalism – with its emphasis on *submission* to the narrow verdict of the market and on the *justice* of the status quo – is inimical to the exercise and enrichment of free will.

If we value free will, then we must promote and protect the conditions that strengthen and sustain effective choice-making – better education, accurate information (rather than the systemic deception of advertising and politics), a supportive society, a workplace that encourages rather than stifles creative choices and exploration and the exercise of autonomous control. Philosophers typically undervalue the *mundane* exercise of free will, the vitally important choice and control that occurs at home and at work, in school and our social lives, and in long-term care facilities. Such workaday choices are vital to our psychological well-being and to maintaining and strengthening our capacity for free will. Loss of control over commonplace everyday choices leads to depression, greater vulnerability to infection, and a higher mortality rate (Bandura et al. 1988; Langer and Rodin 1976; Rodin 1986; Rodin and Langer 1977; Schorr and Rodin 1982; Schulz 1976; Schulz and Hanusa 1978; Wallston 1993).

Support and encouragement for exercising choice and control in our daily lives is not only psychologically healthy but also essential for strengthening our powers of effective choice and control in our larger decisions as well as in the political sphere. Neoliberalism prefers citizens who *submissively* accept the judgment of the market and the orders of their superiors. Moral responsibility molds the submissive citizens valued by neoliberalism. Shaping active and effective citizens of a genuine participatory democracy requires a free will that is daily nurtured and protected and promoted and a free will that rejects the choice-inhibiting effects of moral responsibility.

Conclusion

The history of American proto-neoliberalism and contemporary neoliberalism is dark and discouraging, but there are some positive American elements that are grounds for optimism – the *ideals* that America has celebrated but never followed are powerful shared values for most Americans, no matter how egregiously they have been betrayed by the American elite from the founders to the present. Those ideals are inspiring, and widely shared – real freedom of opportunity; liberty and justice for all; a true democracy, governed by the people and for the people. These goals have never been achieved and have rarely been sincerely pursued, but that does not lessen their value as worthwhile goals. Contemporary feminists have shown the absurdity of radical individualism and "self-made men" as well as the fundamental importance of family and community, and shared goals could help overcome the radical individualism, heal the deep divisions, and unite us. But first, we must look in the mirror and face our own contributions to this deep divisiveness: the lack of respect – even contempt – for the essential hard-working people whose skills and intelligence and diligence make our lives livable. If neoliberalism is to be defeated, that will require a cooperative effort among the full range of working people: plumbers and professors and nurses and construction workers and truck drivers. The essential first step in achieving that cooperation is sincere appreciation and respect for the contributions and struggles and intelligence and autonomy of those who are not our college friends.

REFERENCES

Acharya, Avidit, Matthew Blackwell, and Maya Sen. 2016. "The Political Legacy of American Slavery." *Journal of Politics* 78 (3):621–641. doi: 10.1086/686631.

Adamson, Christopher R. 1983. "Punishment after Slavery: Southern State Penal Systems, 1865–1890." *Social Problems* 30 (5):555–569.

Alesina, Alberto, and Edward L. Glaeser. 2004. *Fighting Poverty in the US and Europe*. Oxford: Oxford University Press.

Alesina, Alberto, Stefanie Stantcheva, and Edoardo Teso. 2018. "Intergenerational Mobility and Preferences for Redistribution." *American Economic Review* 108 (2):521–554. doi: http://www.aeaweb.org/aer/.

Amnesty International. 2012. Cruel Isolation: Amnesty International's Concerns about Conditions in Arizona Maximum Security Prisons.

Arrigo, Bruce A., and Jennifer Leslie Bullock. 2008. "The Psychological Effects of Solitary Confinement on Prisoners in Supermax Units: Reviewing What We Know and Recommending What Should Change." *International Journal of Offender Therapy and Comparative Criminology* 52 (6):622–640. doi: 10.1177/0306624X07309720.

Augustine. 1957. *Saint Augustine Against Julian*. Translated by Matthew A. Schumacher. New York: Fathers of the Church.

Babb, Sarah, and Alexander Kentikelenis. 2018. "International Financial Institutions as Agents of Neoliberalism." In *The SAGE Handbook of Neoliberalism*, edited by Damien Cahill, Melinda Cooper, Martijn Konings and David Primrose, 16–27. Thousand Oaks, California: SAGE Publications.

Babcock, Charles R., and Patrick Tyler. 1981. "Fired U.S. Waste-Fighters Bare Government Foulups," *Washington Post*, February 2, 1981.

Bandura, Albert. 1997. *Self-Efficacy: Toward a Unifying Theory of Behavioral Change*. New York: W. H. Freeman.

Bandura, Albert, Delia Cioffi, C. Barr Taylor, and Mary E. Brouillard. 1988. "Perceived Self-Efficacy in Coping with Cognitive Stressors and Opioid Activation." *Journal of Personality and Social Psychology* 55 (3):479–488. doi: 10.1037/0022-3514.55.3.479.

Bazzi, Samuel, Martin Fiszbein, and Mesay Gebresilasse. 2017. "Frontier Culture: The Roots and Persistence of'FrontierCculture' in the United States." National Bureau of Economic Research, Working Paper 23997. Doi: 10.3386/w23997.

Beckett, Katherine. 1997. *Making Crime Pay: Law and Order in Contemporary American Politics*. New York: Oxford University Press.

Berlin, Isaiah. 1969. "Two Concepts of Liberty." In *Four Essays on Liberty*, edited by Isaiah Berlin. London: Oxford University Press.

Bersot, Heather Y., and Bruce A. Arrigo. 2010. "Inmate Mental Health, Solitary Confinement, and Cruel and Unusual Punishment: An Ethical and Justice Policy Inquiry." *Journal of Theoretical & Philosophical Criminology* 2 (3):1–82.

Bivens, Josh, Elise Gould, Lawrence Mishel, and Heidi Shierholz. 2014. "Raising America's Pay: Why It's our Central Economic Policy Challenge." Economic Policy Institute, Briefing Paper #378. https://www.epi.org/publication/raising-americas-pay/.

Bjork, James M., and Daniel W. Hommer. 2007. "Anticipating Instrumentally Obtained and Passively-Received Rewards: A Factorial fMRI Investigation." *Behavioural Brain Research* 177 (1):165–170. doi: 10.1016/j.bbr.2006.10.034.

Blackmon, Douglas A. 2008. *Slavery by Another Name: The Re-Enslavement of Black Americans from the Civil War to World War II*. New York: Random House.

Boaler, Jo. 2008. "Promoting 'RelationalEequity' and High Mathematics Achievement through an Innovative Mixed-Ability Approach." *British Educational Research Journal* 34 (2):167–194. doi: 10.1080/01411920701532145.

Bodek, Norman. 2011. "*Zenjidoka*, Solving Toyota's Quality Problems." *Quality Digest*.

Bown, Nicola J., Daniel Read, and Barbara Summers. 2003. "The Lure of Choice." 16 (4):297–308. doi: doi:10.1002/bdm.447.

Brembs, Björn. 2010. "Towards a Scientific Concept of Free Will as a Biological Trait: Spontaneous Actions and Decision-Making in Invertebrates." *Proceedings of the Royal Society B: Biological Sciences* doi: 10.1098/rspb.2010.2325%J.

Brown, Wendy. 2019. *In the Ruins of Neoliberalism*. New York: Columbia University Press.

Brownson, Orestes. 1840. "The Laboring Classes." *Boston Quarterly Review* 3:385–395.

Burak, Esra. 2013. "The Social Maximum: American Attitudes toward Extremely High Incomes." *Research in Social Stratification and Mobility* 31 (6):97–114.

Burkhauser, Richard V., Shuaizhang Feng, Stephen P. Jenkins, and Jeff Larrimore. 2012. "Recent Trends in Top Income Shares in the United States: Reconciling Estimates from March CPS and IRS Tax Return Data." *Review of Economics and Statistics* 94 (2):371–388. doi: http://www.mitpressjournals.org/loi/rest.

Cacioppo, John T., and Richard E. Petty. 1982. "The Need for Cognition." *Journal of Personality and Social Psychology* 42 (1):116–131. doi: 10.1037/0022-3514.42.1.116.

Cacioppo, John T., Richard E. Petty, Jeffrey A. Feinstein, and W. Blair G. Jarvis. 1996. "Dispositional Differences in Cognitive Motivation: The Life and Times of Individuals Varying in Need for Cognition." *Psychological Bulletin* 119 (2):197–253. doi: 10.1037/0033-2909.119.2.197.

Caldera, Camille G., and Sahar M. Mohammadzadeh. 2019. "Record-Low 4.5 Percent of Harvard College Applicants Accepted to Class of 2023," *The Harvard Crimson*. March 29, 2019. https://www.thecrimson.com/article/2019/3/29/2023-admit-numbers/.

Carey, Jasmine M., and Delroy L. Paulhus. 2013. "Worldview Implications of Believing in Free Will and/or Determinism: Politics, Morality, and Punitiveness." *Journal of Personality* 81 (2):130–141. doi: 10.1111/j.1467-6494.2012.00799.x.

Casella, Jean, and James Ridgeway. 2016. "Introduction." In *Hell Is a Very Small Place*, edited by Jean Casella, James Ridgeway and Sarah Shourd, 16–24. New York: The New Press.

Casler, Krista, and Deborah Kelemen. 2008. "Developmental Continuity in Teleo-Functional Explanation: Reasoning about Nature among Romanian Romani Adults." *Journal of Cognition and Development* 9 (3):340–362. doi: 10.1080/15248370802248556.

Catania, A. Charles, and Terje Sagvolden. 1980. "Preference for Free Choice Over Forced Choice in Pigeons." *Journal of the Experimental Analysis of Behavior* 34 (1):77–86. doi: 10.1901/jeab.1980.34-77.

Cavadino, Michael, and James Dignan. 2006. "Penal Policy and Political Economy." *Criminology & Criminal Justice: An International Journal* 6 (4):435–456. doi: 10.1177/1748895806068581.

Cheney, Dorothy L., and Robert M. Seyfarth. 2007. *Baboon Metaphysics: The Evolution of a Social Mind*. Chicago: University of Chicago Press.

Chetty, Raj, John N. Friedman, Emmanuel Saez, Nicholas Turner, and Danny Yagan. 2017. "Mobility Report Cards: The Role of Colleges in Intergenerational Mobility." National Bureau of Economic Research. Working paper 23618. doi: 10.3386/w23618.

Chipman, Nathaniel. 1793. *Sketches of the Principles of Government, 1793*. Rutland, Vermont: J. Lyon Press.

Chorev, Nitsan. 2005. "The Institutional Project of Neo-Liberal Globalism: The Case of the WTO." *Theory and Society* 34 (3):317–355.

Christie, Nils. 1993. *Crime Control as Industry*. Abingdon, Oxon: Routledge.

Clarke, Simon. 2005. "The Neoliberal Theory of Society." In *Neoliberalism: A Critical Reader*, edited by Alfredo Saad-Filho and Deborah Johnston, 50–59. London: Pluto Press.

Cohen, Arthur R., Ezra Stotland, and Donald M. Wolfe. 1955. "An Experimental Investigation of Need for Cognition." *The Journal of Abnormal and Social Psychology* 51 (2):291–294. doi: 10.1037/H0042761.

Conwell, Russell H. 1915. *Acres of Diamonds*. New York: Harper & Brothers.

Cookson, Peter W., and Caroline Hodges Persell. 1985. *Preparing for Power: America's Elite Boarding Schools*. New York: Basic Books.

Cooper, Melinda. 2017. *Family Values: Between Neoliberalism and the New Social Conservatism*. New York: Zone Books.

Corak, Miles. 2016. "Income Inequality, Social Mobility, and the Decision to Drop Out of High School: Comment." *Brookings Papers on Economic Activity*: 381–385.

Csibra, Gergely, and György Gergely. 1998. "The Teleological Origins of Mentalistic Action Explanations: A Developmental Hypothesis." *Developmental Science* 1 (2):255–259. doi: 10.1111/1467-7687.00039.

Csibra, Gergely, György Gergely, Szilvia Bíró, Orsolya Koós, and Margaret Brockbank. 1999. "Goal Attribution without Agency Cues: The Perception of 'Pure Reason' in Infancy." *Cognition* 72 (3):237–267. doi: 10.1016/S0010-0277(99)00039-6.

Dalbert, Claudia, and Lois A. Yamauchi. 1994. "Belief in a Just World and Attitudes toward Immigrants and Foreign Workers: A Cultural Comparison between Hawaii and Germany." *Journal of Applied Social Psychology* 24 (18):1612–1626. doi: 10.1111/j.1559-1816.1994.tb01565.x.

Davidai, Shai. 2018. "Why Do Americans Believe in Economic Mobility? Economic Inequality, External Attributions of Wealth and Poverty, and the Belief in Economic Mobility." *Journal of Experimental Social Psychology* 79:138–148. doi: 10.1016/j.jesp.2018.07.012.

Davidai, Shai, and Thomas Gilovich. 2015. "Building a More Mobile America–One Income Quintile at a Time." *Perspectives on Psychological Science: A Journal of the Association for Psychological Science* 10 (1):60–71. doi: 10.1177/1745691614562005.

Davidai, Shai, and Thomas Gilovich. 2018. "How Should We Think about Americans' Beliefs about Economic Mobility?" *Judgment & Decision Making* 13 (3):297–304.

Davies, Paul Sheldon. 2019. "Darwinizing Debunking Arguments." *Ratio* 32: 275–289.

Davis, Bruce. 2015. "Just Culture? Just Kidding." *Physicians' Weekly*. May 26, 2015. https://www.physiciansweekly.com/just-culture-just-kidding/.
De Dijn, Annelien. 2020. *Freedom: An Unruly History*. Cambridge, MA: Harvard University Press.
Dehaene, Stanislas. 2014. *Consciousness and the Brain: Deciphering How the Brain Codes Our Thoughts*. New York: Viking.
Dennett, Daniel C. 1984. *Elbow Room: The Varieties of Free Will Worth Wanting*. Cambridge, Massachusetts: The MIT Press.
Dennett, Daniel C. 2003. *Freedom Evolves*. New York: Viking.
Doob, Anthony N., and Julian V. Roberts. 1983. *Sentencing: An Analysis of the Public's View of Sentencing*. Ottawa: Department of Justice, Canada.
Emerson, Ralph Waldo. 1841. "Self-Reliance." In *Essays*. Boston: James Munroe and Company.
Engelhardt, Carina, and Andreas Wagener. 2014. "Biased Perceptions of Income Inequality and Redistribution." CESifo Working Paper Series No. 4838, Available at SSRN: https://ssrn.com/abstract=2463129.
Federal Reserve. 2021. "Distribution of Household Wealth in the U.S. Since 1989." https://www.federalreserve.gov/releases/z1/dataviz/dfa/distribute/table/.
Findley, Keith A. 2011–12. "Adversarial Inquisitions: Rethinking the Search for the Truth." *New York Law School Law Review* 56: 911–941.
Fischer, John Martin. 2007. "Compatibilism." In *Four Views on Free Will*, edited by John Martin Fischer, Robert Kane, Derk Pereboom and Manuel Vargas, 44–84. Malden, MA: Blackwell Publishing.
Fischer, John Martin. 2012. *Deep Control: Essays on Free Will and Value*. New York: Oxford University Press.
Fishkin, James S. 1992. "Bringing Deliberation to Democracy." *Contemporary Philosophy* 14 (2):4–7.
Fiske, Susan T., and Hazel Rose Markus. 2012. *Facing Social Class: How Societal Rank Influences Interaction*. New York: Russell Sage Foundation.
Forman, James. 2017. *Locking Up Our Own: Crime and Punishment in Black America*. New York: Farrar, Straus and Giroux.
Francis, Nathan. 2014. "A Look at Life Inside Norway's Halden Prison, Where there are no Bars and Inmates have Flat-screen TVs Inside their Cells." *Inquisitr*. https://www.inquisitr.com/1550875/a-look-at-life-inside-norways-halden-prison-where-there-are-no-bars-and-inmates-have-flat-screen-tvs-inside-their-cells/.
Frankfurt, Harry G. 1969. "Alternate Possibilities and Moral Responsibility." *Journal of Philosophy* 66 (23):829–839.
Frankfurt, Harry G. 1971. "Freedom of the Will and the Concept of a Person." *Journal of Philosophy* 68 (1):5–20.
Frankfurt, Harry G. 1975. "Three Concepts of Free Action: Part 2." *Aristotelian Society: Supplementary Volume* Suppl 49: 113–125.
Friedman, Milton. 1962. *Capitalism and Freedom*. Chicago: University of Chicago Press.
Friedman, Milton. 1981. "The Invisible Hand in Economics and Politics." Institute of Southeast Asian Studies Singapore, October 14, 1981.
Friedman, Milton, and Rose Friedman. 1980. *Free to Choose: A Personal Statement*. New York: Harcourt.
Furnham, Adrian. 2003. "Belief in a Just World: Research Progress Over the Past Decade." *Personality and Individual Differences* 34 (5):795–817. doi:10.1016/S0191-8869(02)00072-7.

Furnham, Adrian F., and Barrie Gunter. 1984. "Just World Beliefs and Attitudes towards the Poor." *British Journal of Social Psychology* 23 (3):265–269. doi: 10.1111/j.2044-8309.1984.tb00637.x.

Garrett, Brandon L. 2008. "Judging Innocence." *Columbia Law Review* 108 (1):55–142.

Gazzaniga, Michael S. 2011. *Who's in Charge? Free Will and the Science of the Brain*. New York: Ecco.

Goldberg, Lauren. 2006. "Dealing in Debt: The High-Stakes World of Debt Collection after FDCPA." *Southern California Law Review* 79: 711–752.

Gramlich, John. 2019. "Only 2% of Federal Criminal Defendants Go to Trial, and Most Who Do are Found Guilty." Pew Research Center, June 11, 2019. https://www.pewresearch.org/fact-tank/2019/06/11/only-2-of-federal-criminal-defendants-go-to-trial-and-most-who-do-are-found-guilty/.

Grassian, Stuart. 2006. "Psychiatric Effects of Solitary Confinement." *Washington University Journal of Law & Policy* 22 (1):325–383.

Grassian, Stuart. 2008. "Neuropsychiatric Effects of Solitary Confinement." In *The Trauma of Psychological Torture*, edited by Almerindo E. Ojeda, 113–126. Westport, CT: Praeger Publishers/Greenwood Publishing Group.

Guinier, Lani. 2015. *The Tyranny of the Meritocracy: Democratizing Higher Education in America*. Boston: Beacon Press.

Gustafson, Kaaryn. 2009. "The Criminalization of Poverty." *Journal of Criminal Law and Criminology* 99 (3):643–716.

Gustafson, Kaaryn. 2011. *Cheating Welfare: Public Assistance and the Criminalization of Poverty*. New York: New York University Press.

Guyton, John, Patrick Langetieg, Daniel Reck, Max Risch, and Gabriel Zucman. 2021. "Tax Evasion at the Top of the Income Distribution: Theory and Evidence." National Bureau of Economic Research. Working Paper 28542. https://www.nber.org/papers/w28542.

Hafer, Carolyn L., and Laurent Bègue. 2005. "Experimental Research on Just-World Theory: Problems, Developments, and Future Challenges." *Psychological Bulletin* 131 (1):128–167. doi: 10.1037/0033-2909.131.1.128.

Haidt, Jonathan. 2012. *The Righteous Mind: Why Good People Are Divided by Politics and Religion*. New York: Pantheon Books.

Hamann, Trent H. 2009. "Neoliberalism, Governmentality, and Ethics." *Foucault Studies* 6: 37–59.

Harper, David J., and Paul R. Manasse. 1992. "The Just World and the Third World: British Explanations for Poverty Abroad." *The Journal of Social Psychology* 132 (6):783–785. doi: 10.1080/00224545.1992.9712107.

Harris, Don, and Helen C. Muir. 2005. *Contemporary Issues in Human Factors and Aviation Safety*. Aldershot: Ashgate.

Harvey, David. 2005. *A Brief History of Neoliberalism*. New York: Oxford University Press.

Hauser, Oliver P., and Michael I. Norton. 2017. "(Mis)Perceptions of Inequality." *Current Opinion in Psychology* 18:21–25. doi: 10.1016/j.copsyc.2017.07.024.

Hayek, Friedrich A. 1960/2011. *The Constitution of Liberty*. Chicago: University of Chicago Press.

Hayek, Friedrich A. 1976. *Law, Legislation, and Liberty Volume 2: The Mirage of Social Justice*. Vol. 2. Chicago: The University of Chicago Press.

Heisel, Andrew. 2015. "The Rise and Fall of an All-American Catchphrase: 'Free, White, and 21'." *Jezebel*, September 10, 2015.

Hill-HarrisX, The. 2019. "New Poll Finds Overwhelming Support for an Annual Wealth Tax." The Hill. https://thehill.com/hilltv/what-americas-thinking/428747-new-poll-americans-overwhelmingly-support-taxing-the-wealth-of.

Hinton, Elizabeth, and DeAnza Cook. 2021. "The Mass Criminalization of Black Americans: A Historical Overview." *Annual Review of Criminology* 4: 261–286.

Hofstadter, Richard. 1962. *Anti-Intellectualism in American Life*. New York: Random House.

Holborow, Jonathan. 1993. "Interview with Prime Minister John Major, by The Editor." *Mail on Sunday*, February 21.

Holland, Peter. 2011. "The One Hundred Billion Dollar Problem in Small Claims Court: Robo-Signing and Lack of Proof in Debt Buyer Cases." *Journal of Business and Technology Law* 6: 259–286.

Holland, Peter. 2014. "Junk Justice: Statistical Analysis of 4400 Lawsuits by Debt Buyers." *Loyola Consumer Law Review* 26 (2):179–246.

Holland, Peter. 2016. "Current Trends in Consumer Junk Debt Buyer Litigation." *Maryland Bar Journal* 10: 18–27.

Horowitz, Juliana Menasce, Ruth Igielnik, and Rakesh Kochhar. 2020. "Most Americans Say There Is Too Much Economic Inequality in the US, But Fewer Than Half Call It a Top Priority." Pew Research Center. https://www.pewresearch.org/social-trends/2020/01/09/most-americans-say-there-is-too-much-economic-inequality-in-the-u-s-but-fewer-than-half-call-it-a-top-priority/.

Indermaur, David, and Lynne Roberts. 2005. "Perceptions of Crime and Justice." In *Australian Social Attitudes: The First Report*, edited by Shaun Wilson, Rachel Gibson, David Denemark and Mark Western, 141–160. Sydney: UNSW Press.

Indermaur, David, Lynne Roberts, Caroline Spiranovic, Geraldine Mackenzie, and Karen Gelb. 2012. "A Matter of Judgement: The Effect of Information and Deliberation on Public Attitudes to Punishment." *Punishment & Society* 14 (2):147–165.

Innocence Project. 2019. "Informing injustice: The Disturbing Use of Jailhouse Informants." https://innocenceproject.org/informing-injustice/.

Jones, Elizabeth. 2017. "Racism, Fines and Fees and the US Carceral State." *Race & Class* 59 (3):38–50.

Kahan, Dan M. 1998. "Punishment Incommensurability." *Buffalo Criminal Law Review* 1 (2):691–709.

Kahlenberg, Richard D. 2010. "Introduction." In *Affirmative Action for the Rich: Legacy Preferences in College Admissions*, edited by Richard D. Kahlenberg. New York: The Century Foundation Press.

Kahneman, Daniel. 2011. *Thinking, Fast and Slow*. New York: Farrar, Straus and Giroux.

Kalu, Kalu N. 2012. "Elitism, Class and the Democratic Deficit: Founding Themes of the American Republic." In *Global Elites: The Opaque Nature of Transnational Policy Determination*, edited by Andrew Kakabadse and Nada Kakabadse, 127–137. Houndmills, Basingstoke, Hampshire: Palgrave Macmillan.

Kane, Robert. 1985. *Free Will and Values*. Albany, NY: SUNY Press.

Kane, Robert. 1998. *The Significance of Free Will*. New York: Oxford University Press.

Kane, Robert. 2007. "Libertarianism." In *Four Views on Free Will*, edited by Robert Kane John Martin Fischer, Derk Pereboom and Manuel Vargas, 5–43. Malden, MA: Blackwell Publishing.

Kassin, Saul M. 1997. "The Psychology of Confession Evidence." *American Psychologist* 52 (3):221–233.

Kavanau, J. Lee. 1967. "Behavior of Captive White-Footed Mice." *Science* 155 (3770):1632–1639. doi: 10.1126/science.155.3770.1623.

Kelemen, Deborah. 2003. "British and American Children's Preferences for Teleo-Functional Explanations of the Natural World." *Cognition* 88 (2):201–221. doi: 10.1016/S0010-0277(03)00024-6.

Kelemen, Deborah. 2004. "Are Children 'Intuitive Theists'? Reasoning about Purpose and Design in Nature." *Psychological Science* 15 (5):295–301. doi: 10.1111/j.0956-7976.2004.00672.x.

Kelemen, Deborah. 2012. "Teleological Minds: How Natural Intuitions about Agency and Purpose Influence Learning about Evolution." In *Evolution Challenges: Integrating Research and Practice in Teaching and Learning about Evolution*, edited by Sarah K. Brem, Karl S. Rosengren, E. Margaret Evans and Gale M. Sinatra, 66–92. New York: Oxford University Press.

Kelemen, Deborah, and Cara DiYanni. 2005. "Intuitions about Origins: Purpose and Intelligent Design in Children's Reasoning about Nature." *Journal of Cognition and Development* 6 (1):3–31. doi: 10.1207/s15327647jcd0601_2.

Kelemen, Deborah, and Evelyn Rosset. 2009. "The Human Function Compunction: Teleological Explanation in Adults." *Cognition* 111 (1):138–143. doi: 10.1016/j.cognition.2009.01.001.

Kelemen, Deborah, Joshua Rottman, and Rebecca Seston. 2013. "Professional Physical Scientists Display Tenacious Teleological Tendencies: Purpose-Based Reasoning as a Cognitive Default." *Journal of Experimental Psychology: General* 142 (4):1074–1083. doi: 10.1037/a0030399.supp (Supplemental).

Kendall, Diana. 2006. "Class in the United States: Not Only Alive but Reproducing." *Research in Social Stratification and Mobility* 24 (1):89–104. doi: 10.1016/j.rssm.2004.11.001.

Khatri, Naresh, Gordon B. Brown, and Lanis L. Hicks. 2009. "From a Blame Culture to a Just Culture in Health Care." *Health Care Management Review* 34 (4):312–322.

Kiatpongsan, Sorapop, and Michael I. Norton. 2014. "How Much (More) Should CEOs Make? A Universal Desire for More Equal Pay." *Perspectives on Psychological Science* 9 (6):587–593. doi: 10.1177/1745691614549773.

Kitayama, Shinobu, Keiko Ishii, Toshie Imada, Kosuke Takemura, and Jenny Ramaswamy. 2006. "Voluntary Settlement and the Spirit of Independence: Evidence from Japan's 'Northern Frontier'." *Journal of Personality and Social Psychology* 91 (3):369–384. doi: 10.1037/0022-3514.91.3.369.

Klarman, Michael J. 2016. *The Framers' Coup: The Making of the United States Constitution*. New York: Oxford University Press.

Korsgaard, Christine M. 2009. *Self-Constitution: Agency, Identity, and Integrity*. New York: Oxford University Press.

Kraus, Michael W., and Jacinth J. X. Tan. 2015. "Americans Overestimate Social Class Mobility." *Journal of Experimental Social Psychology* 58:101–111. doi: 10.1016/j.jesp.2015.01.005.

Kunda, Ziva, and Steven J. Spencer. 2003. "When Do Stereotypes Come to Mind and When Do They Color Judgment? A Goal-Based Theoretical Framework for Stereotype Activation and Application." *Psychological Bulletin* 129 (4):522–544. doi: 10.1037/0033-2909.129.4.522.

Langer, Ellen J., and Judith Rodin. 1976. "The Effects of Choice and Enhanced Personal Responsibility for the Aged: A Field Experiment in an Institutional Setting." *Journal of Personality and Social Psychology* 34 (2):191–198. doi: 10.1037/0022-3514.34.2.191.

Larson, Edward J. 2004. *Evolution: The Remarkable History of a Scientific Theory*. New York: Random House.

Leape, Lucian L. 1994. "Error in Medicine." *JAMA: Journal of the American Medical Association* 272 (23):1851–1857. doi: 10.1001/jama.272.23.1851.

Lemke, Thomas. 2001. "'The Birth of Bio-politics': Michel Foucault's Lecture at the College De France on Neo-Liberal Governmentality." *Economy and Society* 30 (2):190–207.

Leotti, Lauren A., and Mauricio R. Delgado. 2011. "The Inherent Reward of Choice." *Psychological Science* 22 (10):1310–1318. doi: 10.1177/0956797611417005.

Lerner, Melvin J. 1980. *The Belief in a Just World: A Fundamental Delusion*. New York: Plenum Press.

Lerner, Melvin J., and Dale T. Miller. 1978. "Just World Research and the Attribution Process: Looking Back and Ahead." *Psychological Bulletin* 85 (5):1030–1051. doi: 10.1037/0033-2909.85.5.1030.

Levy, Neil. 2011. *Hard Luck: How Luck Undermines Free Will and Moral Responsibility*. New York: Oxford University Press.

Lewis, C. S. 1971. "The Humanitarian Theory of Punishment." In *Undeceptions: Essays on Theology and Ethics*, edited by C. S. Lewis, 238–249. London: Curtis Brown.

Link, William A. 2008. *Righteous Warrior: Jesse Helms and the Rise of Modern Conservativism*. New York: St. Martin's Press.

Liu, Amy. 2011. "Unraveling the Myth of Meritocracy within the Context of US Higher Education." *Higher Education (00181560)* 62 (4):383–397. doi: 10.1007/s10734-010-9394-7.

Loeffler, Charles E., Jordan Hyatt, and Greg Ridgeway. 2019. "Measuring Self-Reported Wrongful Convictions among Prisoners." *Journal of Quantitative Criminology* 35: 259–286. https://doi.org/10.1007/s10940-018-9381-1.

Lowe, Walter L. 1935. "Free, White, and 21." *The Chicago Defender*.

Luther, Martin. 1823. *On the Bondage of the Will*. Translated by Henry Cole. London: Simpkin and Marshall. Original edition, 1525.

Mackenzie, Geraldine, Nigel Stobbs, Claire Ferguson, and Karen Gelb. 2014. "Measuring the Effects of Small Group Deliberation on Public Attitudes towards Sentencing: Benefits and Challenges." *Current Issues in Criminal Justice* 25 (3):745–761. doi: 10.1080/10345329.2014.12035996.

Macleod, Alistair M. 2007. "Invisible Hand Arguments: Milton Friedman and Adam Smith." *Journal of Scottish Philosophy* 5 (2):103–117. doi: 10.3366/jsp.2007.5.2.103.

Makary, Martin A., and Michael Daniel. 2016. "Medical Error – The Third Leading Cause of Death in the US." 353 *BMJ*. doi: https://doi.org/10.1136/bmj.i2139 (Published 03 May 2016).

Mancini, Matthew J. 1996. *One Dies, Get Another: Convict Leasing in the American South, 1866–1928*. Columbia: University of South Carolina Press.

Manza, Jeff, and Christopher Uggen. 2006. *Locked Out: Felon Disenfranchisement and American Democracy*. New York: Oxford University Press.

Marmaros, David, and Bruce Sacerdote. 2002. "Peer and Social Networks in Job Search." *European Economic Review* 46 (4–5):870–879.

Martinson, Robert. 1974. "What Works? Questions and Answers about Prison Reform." *The Public Interest* 35 (1):22–54.

Mason, Cody. 2013. "International Growth Trends in Prison Privatization." The Sentencing Project. August 20, 2013. https://www.sentencingproject.org/publications/international-growth-trends-in-prison-privatization/.

McCall, Leslie, Derek Burk, Marie Laperrière, and Jennifer A. Richeson. 2017. "Exposure to Rising Inequality Shapes Americans' Opportunity Beliefs and Policy Support." *PNAS Proceedings of the National Academy of Sciences of the United States of America* 114 (36):9593–9598. doi: 10.1073/pnas.1706253114.

Meier, August, and Elliott M. Rudwick. 1966. *From Plantation to Ghetto*. New York: Hill and Wang.

Menkel-Meadow, Carrie. 1996. "The Trouble with the Adversary System in a Postmodern, Multicultural World." *William & Mary Law Review* 38(5): 6–44.

Milgram, Stanley. 1963. "Behavioral Study of Obedience." *The Journal of Abnormal and Social Psychology* 67 (4):371–378. doi: 10.1037/H0040525.

Mills, Rónán, and Jason Frowley. 2014. "Promiscuous Teleology and the Effect of Locus of Control." *The Irish Journal of Psychology* 35 (2–3):121–132. doi: 10.1080/03033910.2015.1011192.

Mishel, Lawrence, and Jori Kandra. 2020. "CEO Compensation Surged 14% in 2019 to $21.3 Million." The Economic Policy Institute. https://www.epi.org/publication/ceo-compensation-surged-14-in-2019-to-21-3-million-ceos-now-earn-320-times-as-much-as-a-typical-worker/.

Montada, Leo. 1998. "Belief in a Just World: A Hybrid of Justice Motive and Self-Interest." In *Responses to Victimizations and Belief in a Just World*, edited by Leo Montada and Melvin Lerner, 217–245. New York: Plenum.

Moore, Michael S. 1997. *Placing Blame: A General Theory of the Criminal Law*. Oxford: Oxford University Press.

Morris, Herbert. 1968. "Persons and Punishment." *Monist* 52:475–501.

Morris, Jenny, and G.T. Royle. 1988. "Offering Patients a Choice of Surgery for Early Breast Cancer: A Reduction in Anxiety and Depression in Patients and Their Husbands." *Social Science & Medicine* 26 (6):583–585. doi: 10.1016/0277-9536(88)90021-4.

Morse, Stephen J. 1984. "Undiminished Confusion in Diminished Capacity." *Journal of Criminal Law & Criminology* 75 (1):1–55. doi: 10.2307/1143205.

Moyn, Samuel. 2018. *Not Enough: Human Rights in an Unequal World*. Cambridge, MA: Harvard University Press.

Nagel, Thomas. 1979. *Mortal Questions*. Cambridge: Cambridge University Press.

Nair, Unnikrishnan, and S. Ramnarayan. 2000. "Individual Differences in Need for Cognition and Complex Problem Solving." *Journal of Research in Personality* 34:305–328.

Natapoff, Alexandra. 2006. "Beyond Unreliable: How Snitches Contribute to Wrongful Convictions." *Golden Gate University Law Review* 37 (1):107–129.

National Registry of Exonerations 2019 Annual Report. 2020. https://www.law.umich.edu/special/exoneration/Documents/Exonerations_in_2019.pdf.

New York City Bar Association Committee on International Human Rights. 2011. Supermax Confinement in U.S. Prisons. New York.

Niehues, J. 2014. "Subjective Perceptions of Inequality and Redistributive Preferences: An International Comparison." German Economic Institute. IW Trends Number 2. June 25, 2014. https://www.iwkoeln.de/en/studies/iw-trends/beitrag/judith-niehues-subjektive-ungleichheitswahrnehmung-und-umverteilungspraeferenzen-175257.html.

Nietzsche, Friedrich Wilhelm. 1966. *Beyond Good and Evil: Prelude to a Philosophy of the Future*. Translated by Walter Kaufmann. New York: Vintage Books. Original edition, 1886.

Noll, Mark A. 1992. *A History of Christianity in the United States and Canada*. Grand Rapids, Michigan: Wm. B. Eerdmans Publishing Co.

Norton, Michael I., and Dan Ariely. 2011. "Building a Better America-One Wealth Quintile at a Time." *Perspectives on Psychological Science* 6 (1):9–12. doi: 10.1177/1745691610393524.

Nosek, Brian A., Frederick L. Smyth, Jeffrey J. Hansen, Thierry Devos, Nicole M. Lindner, Kate A. Ranganath, Colin Tucker Smith, Kristina R. Olson, Dolly Chugh, Anthony G. Greenwald, and Mahzarin R. Banaji. 2007. "Pervasiveness and Correlates of Implicit Attitudes and Stereotypes." *European Review of Social Psychology* 18:36–88. doi: 10.1080/10463280701489053.

OECD. 2011. *Divided We Stand: Why Inequality Keeps Rising*. Paris: OECD Publishing. https://read.oecd-ilibrary.org/social-issues-migration-health/the-causes-of-growing-inequalities-in-oecd-countries_9789264119536-en#page3.

Olson, Kenneth, Cameron Camp, and Dana Fuller. 1984. "Curiosity and Need for Cognition." *Psychological Reports* 54 (1):71–74. doi: 10.2466/pr0.1984.54.1.71.

Osberg, Timothy M. 1987. "The Convergent and Discriminant Validity of the Need for Cognition Scale." *Journal of Personality Assessment* 51 (3):441–450. doi: 10.1207/s15327752jpa5103_11.

Oshinsky, David M. 1996. *Worse Than Slavery: Parchman Farm and the Ordeal of Jim Crow Justice*. New York: Simon & Schuster.

Paris, Margaret L. 1997. "Lying to Ourselves." *Oregon Law Review* 76 (4):817–832.

Peebles, Gustav. 2013. "Washing Away the Sins of Debt: The Nineteenth-Century Eradication of the Debtors' Prison." *Comparative Studies in Society and History* 55 (3):701–724.

Pellegrino, Edmund D. 2004. "Prevention of Medical Error: Where Professional and Organizational Ethics Meet." In *Accountability: Patient Safety and Policy Reform*, edited by Virginia A. Sharpe, 83–98. Washington, D.C: Georgetown University Press.

Pew Research Center. 2012. "Partisan Polarization Surges in Bush, Obama Years." https://www.pewresearch.org/politics/2012/06/04/partisan-polarization-surges-in-bush-obama-years/.

Pickard, Hanna. 2011. "Responsibility without Blame: Empathy and the Effective Treatment of Personality Disorder." *Philosophy, Psychiatry, & Psychology* 18 (3):209–223. doi: 10.1353/ppp.2011.0032.

Piff, Paul K., et al. 2010. "Having Less, Giving More: The Influence of Social Class on Prosocial Behavior." *Journal of Personality and Social Psychology* 99:771–784.

Piketty, Thomas. 2017. *Capital in the Twenty-First Century*. Translated by Arthur Goldhammer. Cambridge, MA: Harvard University Press.

Piketty, Thomas. 2020. *Capital and Ideology*. Translated by Arthur Goldhammer. Cambridge, MA: Harvard University Press.

Piketty, Thomas, and Emmanuel Saez. 2001. *Income Inequality in the United States, 1913–1998, NBER Working Paper Series: no. 8467*: National Bureau of Economic Research. https://www.nber.org/system/files/working_papers/w8467/w8467.pdf?ncid=txtlnkusaolp00000603.

Raeder, Myrna S. 2007. "See No Evil: Wrongful Convictions and the Prosecutorial Ethics of Offering Testimony by Jailhouse Informants and Dishonest Experts." *Fordham Law Review* 76 (3):1413–1452.

Raine, Adrian. 2013. *The Anatomy of Violence: The Biological Roots of Crime*. New York: Pantheon Books.

Roberts, Lynne D., and David Indermaur. 2007. "Predicting Punitive Attitudes in Australia." *Psychiatry, Psychology & Law* 14 (1):56–65. doi: 10.1375/pplt.14.1.56.

Rodin, Judith. 1986. "Aging and Health: Effects of the Sense of Control." *Science* 233 (4770):1271–1276. doi: 10.1126/science.3749877.

Rodin, Judith, and Ellen J. Langer. 1977. "Long-Term Effects of a Control-Relevant Intervention with the Institutionalized Aged." *Journal of Personality and Social Psychology* 35 (12):897–902. doi: 10.1037//0022-3514.35.12.897.

Roskies, Adina L. 2012. "Don't Panic: Self-Authorship without Obscure Metaphysics." *Nous-Supplement: Philosophical Perspectives* 26:323–342.

Roth, Jessica A. 2016. "Informant Witnesses and the Risk of Wrongful Convictions." *American Criminal Law Review* 53:737–797.

Sabadish, Natalie, and Lawrence Mishel. 2013. "CEO Pay in 2012 Was Extraordinarily High Relative to Typical Workers and Other High Earners." Economic Policy Institute. https://www.epi.org/publication/ceo-pay-2012-extraordinarily-high/.

Sabatini, Nicholas A. 2008. "Reaching the Next Level of Aviation Safety." *FAASTeam News* (Federal Aviation Administration – FAASTeam – FAASafety.gov).

Salzberg, Sharon. 2010. "Buddhism: Between Desire and Emptiness." *Huffington Post.*

Saunders, Daniel B. 2010. "Neoliberal Ideology and Public Higher Education in the United States." *Journal for Critical Education Policy Studies (JCEPS)* 8 (1):41–77.

Schachner, Adena, Liqi Zhu, Jing Li, and Deborah Kelemen. 2017. "Is the Bias for Function-Based Explanations Culturally Universal? Children from China Endorse Teleological Explanations of Natural Phenomena." *Journal of Experimental Child Psychology* 157:29–48. doi: 10.1016/j.jecp.2016.12.006.

Schorr, Dennis, and Judith Rodin. 1982. "The Role of Perceived Control in Practitioner-Patient Relationships." In *Basic Processes in Helping Relationships*, edited by T. A. Willis, 155–186. New York: Academic Press.

Schulz, R. 1976. "Effects of Control and Predictability on the Physical and Psychological Well-Being of the Institutionalized Aged." *Journal of Personality and Social Psychology* 33 (5):563–573. doi: 10.1037//0022-3514.33.5.563.

Schulz, Richard, and Barbara H. Hanusa. 1978. "Long-Term Effects of Control and Predictability-Enhancing Interventions: Findings and Ethical Issues." *Journal of Personality and Social Psychology* 36 (11):1194–1201. doi: 10.1037/0022-3514.36.11.1194.

Seligman, Martin E. P. 1975. *Helplessness: On Depression, Development, and Death*. New York: W. H. Freeman.

Shamash, Rebecca. 2018. "(Re)Production of the Contemporary Elite through Higher Education: A Review of Critical Scholarship." *Berkeley Review of Education* 8 (1):5–21.

Shephard, Lea Krivinskas. 2011. "Creditor's Contempt." *Brigham Young University Law Review* 2011 (5):1509–1560.

Sher, George. 1987. *Desert*. Princeton, New Jersey: Princeton University Press.

Sher, George. 2006. *In Praise of Blame*. New York: Oxford University Press.

Shimbun, N. K. 1988. *Poka-Yoke: Improving Product Quality by Preventing Defects*. Portland, OR: Productivity Press.

Shingo, S. 1986. *Zero Quality Control: Source Inspection and the Poka-Yoke System*. Portland, OR: Productivity Press.

Simons, Sherri Lee. 2007. "Full Disclosure When Bad Things Happen." *Neonatal Network* 26 (2):131–2. doi: 10.1891/0730-0832.26.2.131.

Shorrock, Steven, Jorg Leonhardt, Tony Licu, and Christoph Peter. 2014. "Systems Thinking for Safety: A White Paper." EUROCONTROL. https://static1.squarespace.com/static/53b78765e4b0949940758017/t/58a132fb725e25197ec72c0d/1517023117381/Shorrock+et+al.++%282014%29+Systems+thinking+for+safety+10+principles+Eurocontrol.pdf.

Sigler, Mary. 2006. "By the Light of Virtue: Prison Rape and the Corruption of Character." *Iowa Law Review* 91 (2):561–607.

Slobodian, Quinn. 2018. *Globalists: The End of Empire and the Birth of Neoliberalism*. Cambridge, Mass: Harvard University Press.

Slobogin, Christopher. 2014. "Lessons from Inquisitorialism." *Southern California Law Review* 87: 699–731.

Smith, Adam. 1993. *An Inquiry into the Nature and Causes of the Wealth of Nations*. Oxford: Oxford University Press. Original edition, 1776.

Soederberg, Susanne. 2013. "The US Debtfare State and the Credit Card Industry: Forging Spaces of Dispossesion." *Antipode* 45 (2):493–512.
Spiranovic, Caroline A., Lynne D. Roberts, and David Indermaur. 2012. "What Predicts Punitiveness? An Examination of Predictors of Punitive Attitudes towards Offenders in Australia." *Psychiatry, Psychology & Law* 19 (2):249–261. doi:10.1080/13218719.2011.561766.
Stovall, Tyler. 2021. *White Freedom: The Racial History of an Idea*. Princeton, NJ: Princeton University Press.
Stuntz, William J. 2008. "Inequality and Adversarial Criminal Procedure." *Journal of Institutional and Theoretical Economics* 164: 47–51.
Stuntz, William J. 2011. *The Collapse of American Justice*. Cambridge, MA: Harvard University Press.
Taylor, Charles. 1976. "Responsibility for Self." In *Identities of Persons*, edited by Amelie Rorty, 281–299. Berkeley, California: University of California Press.
Thatcher, Margaret. 1987. *Interview for Woman's Own*. Edited by Douglas Keay. https://www.margaretthatcher.org/document/106689.
Tuomala, Jeffrey C. 1995. "The Value of Punishment: A Response to Judge Richard L. Nygaard." *Regent University Law Review* 5 (1):13–30.
Turner, Frederick Jackson. 1893. "The Significance of the Frontier in American History." American Historical Association, Chicago, July 12, 1893.
Wagstaff, Graham F. 1983. "Correlates of the Just World in Britain." *The Journal of Social Psychology* 121 (1):145–146. doi: 10.1080/00224545.1983.9924476.
Waller, Bruce N. 1989. "From Hemlock to Lethal Injection: The Case for Self-Execution." *International Journal of Applied Philosophy* 4 (4):53–58.
Waller, Bruce N. 2004. "Neglected Psychological Elements of Free Will." *Philosophy, Psychiatry, and Psychology* 11 (2):111–118.
Waller, Bruce N. 2011. *Against Moral Responsibility*. Cambridge, Massachusetts: The MIT Press.
Waller, Bruce N. 2015. *Restorative Free Will: Back to the Biological Base*. Lanham, MD: Lexington.
Wallston, Kenneth A. 1993. "Psychological Control and Its Impact in the Management of Rheumatological Disorders." *Baillière's Clinical Rheumatology* 7 (2):281–295. doi: 10.1016/S0950-3579(05)80090-1.
Wamsley, Dillon. 2019. "Neoliberalism, Mass Incarceration, and the US Debt-Criminal Justice Complex." *Critical Social Policy* 39 (2):248–267.
Wang, Long, and J. Keith Murnighan. 2014. "Money, Emotions, and Ethics Across Individuals and Countries." *Journal of Business Ethics* 125 (1):163–176.
White House, Office of the Press Secretary. 2012. Remarks by the President at a Campaign Event in Roanoke, Virginia, July 13.
Whyte, Jessica. 2019a. *The Morals of the Market: Human Rights and the Rise of Neoliberalism*. London: Verso.
Whyte, Jessica. 2019b. "The Invisible Hand of Friedrich Hayek: Submission and Spontaneous Order." *Political Theory* 47 (2):156–184.
Williams, Bernard. 1981. *Moral Luck*. Cambridge: Cambridge University Press.
Williams, Bernard. 1993. *Shame and Necessity*. Berkeley, California: University of California Press.
Wilson, James Q. 1998. "Selective Incapacitation." In *Principled Sentencing: Readings on Theory and Policy*, edited by Andrew von Hirsch and Andrew J. Ashworth, 113–120. Oxford: Hart Publishing.
Wilson, Timothy D. 2002. *Strangers to Ourselves: Discovering the Adaptive Unconscious*. Cambridge, MA: Harvard University Press.

Wojcieszak, Doug, John Banja, and Carole Houk. 2006. "The Sorry Works! Coalition: Making the Case for Full Disclosure." *Joint Commission Journal on Quality and Patient Safety* 32 (6):344–50. doi: 10.1016/s1553-7250(06)32044-2.

Wolf, Susan. 1990. *Freedom Within Reason*. Oxford: Oxford University Press.

Wolff, Jonathan, and Avner De-Shalit. 2007. *Disadvantage*. Oxford: Oxford University Press.

Young, Michael. 2001. "Down with Meritocracy." *The Guardian*. Accessed December 31, 2020. https://www.theguardian.com/politics/2001/jun/29/comment.

Younis, Mohamed. 2019. "Four in 10 Americans Embrace Some Form of Socialism." May 20, 2019. https://news.gallup.com/poll/257639/four-americans-embrace-form-socialism.aspx.

Zywicki, Todd J. 2003. "The Past, Present, and Future of Bankruptcy Law in America." *Michigan Law Review* 101 (6):2016–2036. doi: 10.2307/3595342.

INDEX

Page references followed by "n" denote notes.

For Product Safety Concerns and Information please contact our EU
representative GPSR@taylorandfrancis.com
Taylor & Francis Verlag GmbH, Kaufingerstraße 24, 80331 München, Germany

www.ingramcontent.com/pod-product-compliance
Ingram Content Group UK Ltd.
Pitfield, Milton Keynes, MK11 3LW, UK
UKHW022355190926
475702UK00015B/2309

* 9 7 8 1 0 3 2 2 5 7 1 5 0 *